PEBBLES FROM MY SKULL

Pebbles from My Skull

STUART HOOD

faber and faber

This edition first published in 2013
by Faber and Faber Ltd
Bloomsbury House, 74–77 Great Russell Street
London WC1B 3DA

Printed and bound by CPI Group (UK) Ltd, Croydon, CR0 4YY

All rights reserved
© Stuart Hood, 1963, 1984
Preface to the 2013 Edition and chronology © Svetlana Hood, 2013

The right of Stuart Hood to be identified
as author of this work has been asserted in accordance
with Section 77 of the Copyright, Designs and Patents Act 1988

This book is sold subject to the condition that it shall not, by way of
trade or otherwise, be lent, resold, hired out or otherwise circulated
without the publisher's prior consent in any form of binding or cover other than
that in which it is published and without a similar condition including this
condition being imposed on the subsequent purchaser

A CIP record for this book is available from the British Library

ISBN 978-0-571-29623-1

Contents

Preface to the 2013 Edition   1
Stuart Hood: A Chronology   6
Prologue   9
The Savage Wood   15
The Sweet Season   89
Epilogue   132
Afterword   136

Preface to the 2013 Edition

Fifty years ago Hutchinson brought out the first edition of *Pebbles from My Skull*. This reissue coincides with the seventieth anniversary of the Italian Armistice – in short, the surrender of Italy to the Allied Forces on 8 September 1943 and the beginning of the long, uncertain and torturous path towards the total liberation of Italy and Europe from Fascism. It coincides also with Captain Stuart Hood's escape on 9 September from one of the seventy-two POW camps in Italy – the PG49, based in the village of Fontanellato di Parma. Over four hundred officers, captured in the African desert, left the converted orphanage in Fontanellato – the Italian camp commander, who aided the escape, was sent to a concentration camp in Germany.

The armistice was followed by a mass-escape of prisoners-of-war. Some historians describe it as 'the greatest mass-escape in history'. Of a total population of some 80,000 prisoners-of-war in Italian hands, approximately 50,000 had the chance to leave their camps. They came from a variety of nationalities and backgrounds. Only one in four of those who emerged from the camps would escape recapture. Most made their way south and through the Allied lines; some were recaptured and shipped to Germany. Others were never heard of again – shot or killed, drowned, lost.

To a large extent the peasant population supported and sustained the floating population of escapees and guerrilla fighters. This was a crucial alliance which benefited both parties but which had many risks attached to it. Captain Edward Mumford and Captain Stuart Hood decided to embark together on a long walk that took them over the Emilian Apennines into Tuscany. They always relied on this alliance for their survival.

Pebbles from My Skull

Along the way they encountered partisan and guerrilla fighters. At times they turned into such fighters themselves. The first encounter was on Monte Morello, in the hills above Florence. For three weeks Captain Mumford and Captain Hood joined a heterogeneous group. From the beginning it was evident that the group did not have proper military training and their political thinking was 'unsophisticated'. The leadership was poor. Captain Hood received the *nom de guerre* 'Carlino'.

On 3 January the majority of the members of the group were sleeping in a hut on Monte Calvana (at the hamlet of Valibona), with no sentries, when they were attacked by a group of local fascist militia. In the skirmish the resistance group was almost annihilated – most of their guns did not work properly. Captain Hood escaped but had to go underground and resume his life as an escaped prisoner of war, relying again on the support of the local peasants. Captain Mumford, who at the time of the skirmish was away, decided to go up north and eventually managed to cross the frontier into Switzerland.

In mid-March Captain Hood reached Chianti, a few miles from Siena. He joined the Raggruppamento Patrioti Monte Amiata. It was a fairly large and well-organised military formation with good grounding in guerrilla warfare. Its commanders were ex-high-ranking Italian officers. Many were of aristocratic descent. Most of the officers belonged to or were sympathisers of the very progressive Action Party. The political and tactical discussions were of high level. Captain Hood became guerrilla fighter *Capitano* Hood and was put in charge of one of the thirty-two-plus platoons. He carried out a number of military operations and helped to liaise with other local insurgents. On 27 June, *Capitano* Hood was given a new identity – 'Luigi Neri', member of the Polizia Urbana – and sent to Siena to help to prepare the ground for the arrival of the Allied forces.

It is accepted that the Italian Resistance had some 100,000 active members. Of these, around half died or were sent to concentration camps, and one-third of them were injured or mutilated. These figures exceed those sustained by regular armed forces. Historians are divided as to the military

Preface to the 2013 Edition

achievements of the Resistance. There is, however, more consensus as to their political attainments. In Paul Ginsborg's words, 'The Resistance's aspirations to a more direct and socially just form of democracy and state, aspirations shared by most Socialist, Communist and Action Party members alike, were not to be realised.'

The story of escape and survival told in *Pebbles from My Skull* is not an anthropological description of peasant life in the strict sense of the term. It is not a chronological account of the adventures of an escapee turned (at times) guerrilla fighter, although it has occasional elements of the same. No diaries were kept and therefore the recollections could not be cross-referenced. No interviews were carried out and so the data could not be compared or verified. Captain Mumford and Captain Hood did not meet prior to the publication of this book – and when they met in the late 1980s their recollections differed in many respects.

Stuart Hood made several attempts to write a book about his time in Italy. All attempts, in his view, failed. Finally, and following a lengthy course of psychoanalysis, the key existential question became apparent: 'Why did it take me from the 8 September 1943 to 15 August 1944 to cross the line, reassume my identity, step back out of limbo?' The search for answers allowed him to reassess meaningfully his time as an escapee, to understand better the nature of the experience he went through and the complexities – methodological and philosophical – of writing a piece of autobiographical work. Thus in the words of the Hutchinson editors, 'His book is no blood-and-thunder record of adventure. It is contemplative reflection.'

The philosophical dilemmas of this contemplative reflection are formulated almost poetically by Friedrich Nietzsche in Prologue 1 to *On the Genealogy of Morals*:

> Imagine someone who, when woken suddenly from divine distraction and self-absorption by the twelve loud strokes of the noon bell, asks himself: 'What time is it?' In much the same way, we rub our ears *after the fact* and ask in complete surprise and embarrassment: '*What* was that we

Pebbles from My Skull

just experienced?', or even 'Who *are* we really?' Then we count back over in retrospect, as I said, every one of the twelve trembling strokes of our experience, our life, our *being* – and alas! lose our count in the process ... And so we necessarily remain a mystery to ourselves, we fail to understand ourselves, we are *bound* to mistake ourselves.

Stuart Hood concludes his book with a definition and a warning along the similar lines: 'Autobiography is an attempted jail-break. The reader tunnels through the same dark'.

Acknowledgments

On the commemoration of the sixtieth anniversary of the Italian Armistice the few surviving members of the PG49 met at the old camp for the last time. They assessed the events, shared their memories and to some extent reenacted their escape and retraced the various routes taken. Now all their memories, oral and written, are in the hands of the historians. In the last few years a new wave of local and specialised historical work has been undertaken. New insights have been gained. However, a comprehensive and critical view of the war in Italy – 'a brutal history', as Richard Lamb called it – has yet to emerge.

The group agreed that a special recognition and gratitude should be given to all the Italians who sheltered and fed them – regardless of their motives; to the enclosed nuns of the Sanctuary of the Most Sacred Rosary of Fontanellato di Parma for all their help and kindness; and to the Red Cross, especially but not solely for the life-enhancing parcels.

Stuart Hood also remembered with special affection and gratitude the commanders of the Raggruppamento Patrioti Monte Amiata, in particular his area commander, Major Guilio Terrosi Vagnoli. He was not only a fair and conscientious land-owner but a very caring and professional commander. He was always concerned about the safety of his guerrilla fighters. In difficult operations he personally took charge of *Capitano* Hood's platoon, risking his own life. Stuart Hood explained that on the Major Terrosi's estate he felt at long last more at

Preface to the 2013 Edition

ease with himself: the Major's tenants helped him to look to the future with a degree of hope – hence the title of the chapter dealing with this period, 'Sweet Season'. After the war, Stuart Hood regularly returned to this most beautiful spot in Chianti in search of that elusive moment in the past – the irony was that the estate had been sold to a German financier.

Finally but most importantly his gratitude went to Captain Edward Mumford – his most kind and generous companion. Stuart Hood said that their relationship was rather like rock-climbing: 'You climb with someone and you have total confidence in them, though you might have nothing in common apart from that piece of rock. I had immense confidence in him'.

Svetlana Hood
(social scientist, and Stuart Hood's
collaborator and wife for over
three decades), September 2013

Stuart Hood: A Chronology

17 December 1915	Birth of Stuart Hood in Edzell, Angus, Scotland (a farming and fishing community). His parents were Presbyterian. His father was headmaster of the local primary school.
1933	Receives medals for high achievement in German, French and Latin from the Montrose Academy.
1934–38	Edinburgh University: studies for a degree in English and undertakes formal training in Russian language and culture at evening classes. Joins the Communist Youth. (Resigns in 1940. Does not join the Communist Party after the war – instead, supports and works with the Russian dissidents.)
1938	Attains MA (hons) English Literature, Edinburgh University. Classic Italian literature was part of his formal training.
1940–46	Serves in the British Army.
1940	Volunteers to join the war effort.
1940–42	War service in the Middle East acting as Intelligence Officer.
1942–43	Prisoner of war in Italy – Camp PG49, Fontanellato di Parma.
9 September 1943	Escapes from PG49
December 1943	Reaches Tuscany. Just before Christmas joins a small and badly trained Resistance group operating on the hills above Florence. Receives the *nom de guerre* 'Carlino'.

Stuart Hood: A Chronology

3 January 1944	The group is attacked by a local fascist militia on the Calvana hills – it suffers heavy casualties and is almost annihilated. Stuart Hood escapes. Resumes his life as an escaped prisoner of war.
1944	In March, Hood reaches Chianti. Joins a large and professional Resistance group, Raggruppamento Patrioti Monte Amiata. Its commanders are ex-high-ranking Italian army officers, members or sympathisers of the Action Party. Takes part in high-level political and military discussion. Commands, under the name Capitano Hood, one of its thirty-two-plus platoons. Takes part in sabotage and harassment of German troops, liaises with other groups operating in the area.
27 June 1944	Takes a new identity, Luigi Neri (Polizia Urbana). Moves to Siena.
July 1944	Rejoins the Allied forces in Siena. Travels to Naples.
1944–46	Appointed staff liaison officer with the American 9th Army at Rhine Crossing; subsequently, political intelligence officer in Germany.
1946–64	Employed by the BBC. Starts as sub-editor in the Overseas Service. Becomes successively head of the German and Italian programs; head of the World Service; deputy head of the domestic news services and Editor, Television News; Controller of Programs, BBC TV, responsible for planning the output of BBC 1 and BBC 2. Resigns from the BBC.
1963	Publication of *Pebbles from My Skull*.
1964	Appointed Controller of Programs, Rediffusion Television. Sacked.

Pebbles from My Skull

1965–73	Works as a freelance documentary film-maker, TV scriptwriter, journalist, writer and broadcaster. His output includes: *J. Robert Oppenheimer, The Trial of Daniel and Sinyavsky, Pétain: A Question of Honour*, and *The Chicago Seven*.
1973–78	Appointed Professor of Film and Television at the Royal College of Art. Resigns.
1978–1984	Lectures in media studies.
1985–2011	Becomes an established novelist, author of *Storm from Paradise* (1985), *The Upper Hand* (1987), *The Brutal Heart* (1989), *A Den of Foxes* (1991), *The Book of Judith* (1995). Reworks in fiction some of the themes dealt in his autobiographical work *Pebbles from My Skull*. Becomes a voice critical of the way 'legend' has developed around the Italian Resistance, and in particular of his place in its mythology.
	Lectures and supervises work on creating writing and autobiographical writing
	Translates into English a large number of important European literary work, especially from the Italian.
31 January 2011	Death of Stuart Hood in Brighton, East Sussex, his home for over three decades.

Prologue

Memory is not merely recall. Some things we choose to forget. Some, which we cannot forget, we make bearable. Life washes through us like a tide. In its ebb and flow the fragments of the past are ground smooth so that, with time, we can handle them like stones from a rock pool, admiring their colour, shape and texture. We do not know which of them will stir and rattle as the tide ebbs from us for the last time. These are pebbles from my skull.

A lavatory flushed. A naked figure stalked along the tiled corridor with a spectral motion and disappeared into a dormitory. The water in the cistern played a metallic tune. The sentries in their watch-towers shifted on their feet. Like myself they were waiting to be relieved. When they looked up they could see me at the attic window. I knew they would not fire as once they might have done. Things had gone too far, become too complicated. It was four o'clock on the morning of 9 September 1943.

The reliefs came clattering out of the guardroom, clumsily slung their old-fashioned rifles, and walked off between the inner and outer wire, crunching the gravel. Mine came softly up the stair and asked: 'Anything?' 'Nothing.' Together we sat on the window-sill and looked out over the plain. The orphanage, our prison, stood on the edge of the village. It backed on to the fields. There was a double barrier of wire between them and us. The white blobs on the wire were flowers. You could choose what name to call them: bindweed or traveller's joy.

To our left, behind their high blind wall, lived the

Pebbles from My Skull

enclosed nuns who kept the village shrine — the Sanctuary of the Most Sacred Rosary of Fontanellato di Parma. They did our laundry. We sent them, for their pains, little notes of thanks or trifling gifts from the Red Cross parcels — a cake of soap, a bar of chocolate, tea, wrapped in a shirt or the fading drill shorts of the desert war. They rang the bells that woke us in the morning before sunrise and set the cigarettes glowing and waning in the early dark. On 15 August, the great festival, they had made the bells peal for a night and a day in honour of the Blessed Virgin and her Assumption. We cursed their jangling as we sat in the sun beside the wire and watched the holiday girls cycle past with skirts ballooning over their knees.

On our right, another blind wall, whitewashed, pale in the darkness. In it, in their narrow niches, the village dead lay immured like grubs in a honeycomb. Beyond the cemetery a dusty road split into two white ribbons. One ran south to the railway and the Via Emilia — that way the Germans would come. The other ran north to Busseto, six miles away, where Verdi was born, and to the unfordable, unswimmable, uncrossable Po.

Once a week we passed through the barrier for a walk under escort: a mile out and back in column of threes. The guards trotted along beside us in their patched boots. Their long, antiquated rifles bobbed at all angles. It was the height of wit to pluck, when we halted, a sprig of clover or a daisy and plant it in a rusty muzzle. So we took our small revenges as we strode out, marching the short-rumped, fourth category guards off their feet. The metalled roads were thick with dust. There was living water everywhere in ditches and irrigation canals. The trees and bushes were full of nightingales. A well-kept cottage said on its gate: *Parva sed apta mihi*. Some retired schoolmaster. Of the village itself we knew only a single straggling street. There was a little shop selling bread and groceries. Another, beside the convent, full of candlesticks and *bondieuserie*. A mottled grey war memorial, heavy with rhetoric and broken swords. An alley of trees where on feast days the travelling

Prologue

fairs set up roundabouts, shooting galleries with tinsel prizes, booths for hot doughnuts, booths for cold pork stuck with rosemary. Over the convent roof we could see a squat, machicolated tower. We did not know that it stood in an arcaded square with cool, shaded shops and a weekly market: stalls of Parmesan cheese, butter softening in the sun, umbrellas, clodhopper shoes and country clothing. In the keep the officials of the Commune shifted, then as now, the tattered files of Italian bureaucracy. The water of the moat is opaquely green. A few fish stir lazily. Gas bubbles from the ooze.

I went back to my room. Twenty beds. Twenty men who had learned to live together, more or less, and adapt themselves, more or less, to captivity. We fell roughly into three categories. Those whose lives were adjusted to an orderly and not unpleasant routine, such as they had known before in prep or public school. Those who played at escaping — carting spoil from impossible tunnels, conspiring endlessly and fruitlessly. Those who rebelled, who dismissed camp activities — games, discussions, study groups — as opiates; whose motto was the old revolutionary one 'the worse, the better'; who had the revolutionary's patience, lack of scruple and love of mystery. A few were outside any category. They were the ones who had to be watched in case, in broad daylight, they simply got up and jumped the wire. It was difficult to know what they desired more: to escape or to be killed.

We had much in common. In particular the traumatic shock of capture, the uneasy feeling that we should not be alive, the sense of failure. Beyond this, certain memories. The plumed dust thrown up by the attacking armour. Trucks scurrying desperately over the face of the desert. Red points of fire at dusk where the wrecks still burned and glowed under the drooping signal lights. Images of pain, fear or death. A body hanging from the turret of an armoured car like a doll that has lost its sawdust. The

Pebbles from My Skull

confusion of a night battle threaded with tracer. The sensations of extreme heat, extreme cold, hunger and thirst. Names of places and people. The bars, night-clubs and brothels of Cairo. Regimental loyalties, loyalties of place, class and birth. Soon we might be on our own faced with freedom. Freedom meant danger.

As the light grew on the whitewashed walls I tried to cast the balance of our situation. We knew very little. Ever since — in July — an Italian soldier had walked into the camp office, taken Mussolini's picture from the wall and smashed it under foot, we had lived in a kind of limbo, blown about by rumour, wild hope and despondency. We were certain of two things. That the Allies were in the toe of Italy and that there was an armistice — whatever that might mean. We presumed that the Allies would land in the north and nip the peninsula in two. We imagined that the Germans would be moving in, reinforcing, taking over. We did not know whether or not they would be interested in the fate of four hundred officers. There were other imponderables: What would the Italian commandant do? would his men obey him? what were people like outside the wire? how would we react to freedom? how far had captivity unmanned us, limiting our decisions, cushioning us from the world, providing a habitat, an ecology — the corner of a room, a bed, a few books, safety? I had a curious sensation compounded of fear, excitement and expectation. I had felt it before; when I left home for the last time, when the troopship cast off, when I saw the first shell burst on our positions.

To aid me, if it came to the push, I had the normal skills in killing. I had been taught to navigate by the stars, to study terrain, to judge distance, to use my eyes. I could, over and above these things, speak German, Italian and some Russian. I knew rather more about the German army than about my own. I had some skill in interrogation. I knew some tricks. That of two prisoners, the second will probably speak if the other is led away behind a truck and there is a burst of fire. That in such cases no blood need be

Prologue

shed. That fear is a potent weapon. I had read my Italian papers daily, interpreting them with the skills I had learned as an intelligence officer, drawing inferences, finding omissions as revealing as positive statements. I thought I would recognize a revolutionary situation if I saw one. I had a deep belief in the instincts of the common people. I didn't look like an Englishman. I felt that the thing to do was to get up into the foothills of the Apennines and out of the plain. As I dressed, I could see them through the haze, fifteen miles away. My eye picked out a castle tower. It would be a useful landmark.

Uncertainty ended after breakfast. There was a sound of feet running in the corridors, shouts, laughter, commands, the first fumbling notes of a bugle-call. I ran down with the rest into the courtyard.

The Savage Wood

*Ah quanto a dir qual' era è cosa dura
esta selva selvaggia e aspra e forte
che nel pensier rinnova la paura.*

Ah how hard a thing it is to tell of that wood, savage, harsh and dense, the thought of which renews my fear.

Inferno, I, 3–6

1

It is a strange sensation to step into a landscape. For months you have lived like a beetle on a leaf, bound by some tropism to a tiny patch of activity. The landscape has surrounded you on all sides but you have never stepped out into it. So at first you walk warily.

We walked out into the landscape at a bugle-call. It burst along the corridors of our orphanage, leapt the convent wall, flurrying the enclosed nuns, and spread over the plain to the men in the fields and the women on the steadings.

> *Fall in A*
> *Fall in B*
> *Fall in every company*

For the last time we fell in in threes and then, a long straggling group, walked through the fence and into the fields. The watch-towers were empty. By the cemetery wall a couple of guards were siting a light machine-gun to cover the entrance to the village. We followed a little stream. Frogs plopped into the water as we passed. A couple of women walked over to watch us, smiled but did not speak. It was just after midday.

We walked into September and the maize harvest.

In September the cobs make an orange heap on the barn floors. The stalks stand brown and skeletal in the fields, hung with tattered, parchment leaves. The men walk through this insubstantial jungle and clear the land for ploughing. It is easy work and pleasurable, like all licensed destruction. One stroke, well-aimed, cuts the roots out of the earth and the stalk leans over, snapping as it falls. In the barns women and children, old men and vagrants, sit round

Pebbles from My Skull

the piles and strip the cobs. Dry, they will stuff the peasant mattresses. The men in the fields heap the stalks and set them ablaze. The flames are high but almost invisible in the sun. All over the plain the flames rise and sink to a circle of ash. But you can only guess at these other fires, for each field is shut in, fenced off by willows, by the vines looped from trunk to trunk, and by the poplars. This is a landscape lush and claustrophobic, full of water — ditches, rice-fields, irrigation canals — cut by occasional deep gullies (they are thick with acacias and rank herbage), and completely dominated by the sky. In summer that sky is a thin diaphragm stretched taut over the plain, holding and reflecting the heat. In July or August it can darken suddenly; clouds build up to a thunder-head, black below, piling up in white breastworks of ice and hail. The rain moves across the plain in a long grey screen. The thunder drums to and fro. But in September the weather is set and will not change until the grapes are gathered and the ploughing begun. In October it breaks.

The landscape is dominated by the sky. There are a few vantage points: the pale yellow bell-towers of the village churches, a keep rising out of a moated village, a convent or an orphanage. But even from the fourth floor of an orphanage turned prison the prospects barely change. You can see a little further, see a little more green, see yet another bell-tower, something of the foothills, and the pylons where the grid steps over the Po. Really to see the plain you must get out of it, up on to the hills. Then it tilts gently to the horizon, wide and open, cut by a railway and a Roman road, veined with watercourses, patched with villages and town and farmsteads. In the hills you dominate the plain and feel free.

That was one of the reasons why we made for the hills.

We: two men in their late twenties with nothing in common except the shock of capture and the boredom of captivity. When I was born his father was dead — killed at Kut-al-Amarah. Cycling across London to school, he had his life clear before him: Sandhurst and a commission in the

The Savage Wood

Gurkhas. Fatherless, he had learned the practicalities of life. I had mooned away my schooldays, getting by with a certain parrot facility for words. Walking the long bare beaches of the north, I had fantasticated on life, in which I had neither compass nor points of reference. What I knew, I grasped instinctively; what I felt, I did, following my hunches.

Two sets of memories. His of the Frontier, the *jeels* of Kashmir, the mess and the playing-fields. Mine of university politics, milk for Spain, *Battleship Potemkin*, and fine chalk-dust swirling in the class-rooms.

Two different physiques. Ted, broad and powerful, brown, with an Asian look and a thin black moustache, as if he had been assimilated to his own squat soldiers. As we stood in the ranks at morning or evening roll call I looked clean over his head. Myself, tall, thin, sthenic, with a narrow head like a collie-dog's.

We had agreed to make for the hills together. But not right away. For a couple of days we lay in a green gulley, sleeping and planning in the sun. The others disappeared by twos and threes. We sat on in the sun and watched the men clear the maize-fields and planned lazily, discussing the points where the Allies must land — the mouth of the Po, the Riviera, Viareggio — and in a great pincers movement cut the Germans off from the Brenner. If they were delayed more than a few days then we would start walking. Meanwhile we watched by day the men at work in the fields and at night walked over to the nearest farmhouse. It was called Toccalmatto, the madman's lot. The family's name, ironically, was Tedeschi, the Germans.

If you strip life to its essentials they are warmth, food and somewhere to sleep. A peasant house caters for all three needs. Essentially the kitchen is the primeval cave, with at one end a fire of dry brushwood that sends fingers of flame up round the pot, and subsides quickly into a bed of hot ash, grey with a glowing heart. The floor is stone-flagged. In one corner is water carried from the well in copper pitchers, for drinking or washing. From the roof, away from the

Pebbles from My Skull

mice, hang a salami, a home-cured crude ham, and a lump of tallow for greasing boots. The light is a carbide lamp hissing gently over the table. The men sit first and the women serve a thin broth of minestra, or polenta poured like golden lava on to a wooden platter. The bread the man of the house cuts, holding the big flat loaf to his chest and slicing wedges from it with his clasp knife. The wine is harsh. Cheese finishes the meal with maybe a handful of nuts or grapes, or a poor pear or a medlar. In the hearth the brushwood stalks hiss and groan, dripping their sap into the ashes. After supper the fire dies; the lamp begins to flicker; men and women go out singly or in twos to give a last look at the oxen and to relieve their bodies in the byre. Then they turn back to bed.

But those who are not of the household — vagrants, odd men, strangers, boys helping out with the work — sleep with the oxen, which are white, or brindled grey and brown, long-horned, with huge liquid eyes and wet muzzles dripping mucus and saliva. Throughout the night there is a faint clank of chains from their head-stalls, a continual shifting noise as they stir, chew the cud, or dream. From their bellies come long rumbling eructations as they digest the chopped fodder of leaves and grass. Their dung splashes on the floors and flecks the men sleeping in the corner on their bed of sacking and straw. By morning the air is warm and thick from the breath of the beasts; the atmosphere, heavy with ammonia. As you walk out into the yard your eyes stream with tears. A dash of cold water clears your head. In the kitchen the woman is fanning a charcoal stove to boil a pan of thin milk. The children run in and out, hungry, smelling of sleep, urine and unwashed clothes. The man of the house comes in. The oxen have been fed and watered. He is taciturn, turning over in his mind the day's work. Breakfast is home-made bread broken into a bowl of warm milk, sweetened with greyish sugar. The peasant pushes his bowl from him. *Andumma*, he says, let's go.

Day after day we went out into the fields and cut the

The Savage Wood

maize stalks. Our hands hardened and calloused. Our muscles ached and then ceased to ache. One day we admitted to each other that the landings would not come — not quite yet and at midnight we started for the hills.

Our guide was a son of the house. Ted left behind a gold ring saying he would fetch it 'after the war' When we reached the railway line the guide left us. We were in peasant clothes — old jacket and trousers, a collarless shirt. In a sack on our backs we carried our battle-dress. We dropped the sacks over the fence and began to squirm through the wires. They creaked rustily in their staples. Away across the plain a dog barked. We lay, holding our breath and listening. With immense care we dragged our legs through the wire and crawled over the grass verge and on to the ballast. It dug into the joints of the knees. The rail was cool to the touch. I laid my ear on the steel with some childhood memory of listening at a level-crossing for trains far down the line. We crossed the first track. More ballast. The metal tip of my army boot rang against a rail. We crouched waiting for a shout, a challenge, a shot. Far away there were lights — a signal-box or level crossing. We moved on. Grass at last. The second fence we took more carelessly than the first. Then we were on a white dusty road, not talking yet but feeling gay and elated. Through the rest of the night we walked south with the hills rising in front, promising haven. The castle was our landmark.

In the farmyards the dogs woke and rushed, yapping, to and fro. We knew that from their collars a cord went up to a slipring on the wire strung between the eaves of the house and a pole in the corner of the yard. They could not touch us. Geese hissed at us by a pond; ducks stirred on the shadows. Towards dawn a donkey brayed as if caught in some rending orgasm. When daylight was near we chose a barn, dropped down between the straw and the wall and slept.

We were in the hills, safe in the high places from whence cometh our aid. If, a week later, I went back down into the plains, it was a sign that we were beginning to face realities.

Pebbles from My Skull

We would, after all, need a change of socks before the landings.

Our laundry was with the enclosed nuns. From the crest of the hills the two of us looked down and picked out their bell-tower, fifteen miles away beyond the railway and the Roman road. I set off after breakfast, picking my landmarks, hoping to steer a straight course over the plain with its windbreak poplars, its willows, and the sameness of the autumn fields. On the Via Emilia I sat by the roadside and watched the traffic — German trucks and staff-cars with an unfamiliar mottled camouflage. I seemed to attract no notice. Towards midday I passed over the railway at a level crossing. The keeper's wife looked at me curiously. I greeted her and walked on. By one o'clock I was within sight of the village. I was hungry and decided to eat. The precise farmhouse I chose by signs and portents. I liked the look of it. I liked the dog. The man seemed sympathetic. He asked no questions but bade me come in and eat. We talked about the farm and the war. By now my ear was attuned to the Emilian dialect. I was from the north, I said, round about Bolzano, hence my accent. We don't speak Italian here anyway, they said. I thanked them and walked on. No one stood to watch me go — a good augury. I turned to look at the hills. They were a long way back. I was a hundred yards from the end of the village when a bicycle came quietly up behind me in the dust and a man dismounted. The *carabinieri* patrolled on bicycles. I wondered whether to look round or not. The feeling that came over me was a familiar one — memories of it went back to when I lied at home, or was beaten at school, or when an inept surgeon broke the bone of my septum. It was a kind of detachment in which each event had all the time in the world to happen. What I did I did with great deliberation; what happened to me occurred in nightmarish slow motion. From somewhere outside the situation I observed it all. It was a state which frightened me for two reasons — because of the sharp reaction that came hard after it, and because I knew that, while it held, I would be capable of any enormity.

The Savage Wood

The man was walking along just behind me. I could hear the tick of the free-wheel mechanism in the rear hub of his bicycle. He came abreast and spoke. An ordinary peasant, shaven, in his Sunday best, on his way to some family reunion, to see a lawyer, to argue with some bureaucrat. Did I know the way to Busseto? I remembered the escape maps and told him. He thanked me, mounted again and pedalled along quietly by my side. We parted at the crossroads. The village street was empty and white. The siesta. I walked along to the convent church and into the courtyard. There was a Dominican on the steps. 'Father, I have come for my laundry.' He looked at me and said: 'Come into the parlour.'

Three sides of the parlour were wainscotted in brown. A black crucifix and painting of the Virgin — a blue doll with a nodding tiara with another doll in its arms. Somewhere in the Sanctuary the two dolls must stand, in a chapel crammed with *ex voto* plaques — arms, hands, legs, hearts — the graven images of Southern Catholicism, for which I could not feel the true Protestant repugnance; to me they seemed less harmful than those we had invented for ourselves: the father figures of the dictatorships. That they were primitive spoke rather for than against them. The fourth side was a bronze grille. The priest had left me. I was alone. There was a musty smell — a compound of newly washed stone floors, of varnished wood, of airless corridors: the odour of sanctity. From behind the grille came a twittering of voices. I thought I could see white wimples.

What was my laundry number? The voice was young and fresh.

I gave it.
And my friend's?
I gave it too.
Where was he?
In the hills.
The twittering grew louder and more compassionate.
Where did I come from?
Scotland.

Pebbles from My Skull

Where had I learned Italian?
At the university.
Was my mother living?
Yes.
The voices rose and fell in anguish.
Married?
Yes.
Children?
A son.
How old?
Three.
Had I seen him?
No.

There was a noise like birds swarming to rise and circle in the air. In the midst of it all a revolving hatch to one side of the grille swung round to show, one above the other, on its two varnished shelves two bundles: Ted's laundry and my own.

I picked them up and stowed them in my sack, wishing I could find some words, produce some gesture, ask for a blessing, so that they might know my gratitude. I thanked them as best I could and turned to go. There was a flurry behind the grille. Someone ran off down a corridor.

Stay a little.
So I stayed.
We agreed that these were terrible times and that war was horrible.
Where had I been fighting?
In Africa.
A nasty place.
I agreed.
Where had I been captured?
Mersa Matruh.
Was that in Africa too?
Yes, in North Africa.

The shelf revolved again, presenting a glass of vermouth and a plate of thin sponge fingers.

Would I be pleased to taste them?

The Savage Wood

I drank the vermouth slowly and nibbled a sponge finger. From behind the grille they watched in silence. I said how good the fingers were and the vermouth too and thanked them again.

Once more the shelf revolved. A parcel this time — a bag of biscuits for my friend in the hills. I thanked them on his behalf and lifted my sack.

Was I a Christian?

I prevaricated and said I supposed so.

A Catholic?

No.

There was a silence. Then a voice, more authoritative than the others — the Mother Superior's? — said it did not matter.

The shelf rotated for the last time. I gathered from it two cards, cheap pilgrim's reproductions of the blue doll behind me — the Immaculate Virgin of the Sanctuary of Nostro Signora del Santa Rosario. On each, a tiny blue square of silk cut from her robe.

To keep us safe and bring us back to those who loved us.

The Dominican led me back into the street and blessed me on my way.

It was a long walk back. The crossing-keeper's wife waved as I passed. Trucks were still moving on the Via Emilia. I kept my eyes on the castle in the hills and walked. From time to time I stopped and looked at the sponge fingers. They were slightly brittle. I ate the broken bits and went on. On the edge of the plain I stopped to rest before the climb began. I ate the last of Ted's biscuits and threw away the paper bag. Night caught me in the foothills. Cramp set in. I sat and rubbed the muscles till they untensed and then set off again. The stars went behind a cloud, which came creeping over the hilltops. There were a few drops of rain, then a steady drizzle. I had got off the track and was in the middle of ploughed land. On the crest I could see a light which must be our farm. There was no more spring in my knees but I could still crawl. The hill seemed to slope up like a roof. My hand slipped and groped among the slanting

Pebbles from My Skull

furrows. At the field's end I rested and got to my feet again. I walked the last paces to the door.

We needed a change of socks, so I went down into the plain. It was thus that I rationalized a gratuitous act. One sticky Cairo afternoon — it was *Khamsin* weather — I had discussed with H. the relationship between sex and death and my need to confront a situation where my life was in the balance. She told me I had been reading too much Malraux and found the whole idea 'très fasciste'. The same impulse had made me, on the Matruh perimeter, pummel my driver until he drove the jeep among the shell-bursts. It sprang from the desire to test the razor edge of fear. A razor cuts without pain.

2

In the hills we learned about the chestnut harvest and the wine harvest, how to plough and how to use a hoe.

You can walk the Apennines from the plain of Lombardy to far below Florence and almost all the way be among chestnut woods. The mule tracks, branching, climbing, falling between the trees, are slippery with lanceolate leaves; the chestnuts, like green sea-urchins, lie thick among the grass. A mountain girl brings in her dowry a clump of mature trees. In October their fruit is ripe. Long, pliant sticks in their hands, the men clamber barefoot into the branches, balance in a fork with their backs to the trunk, and, leaning out, strike at the clustered fruits, which dance at the tips of the furthest twigs like spiky baubles. The sticks swish and whip at the foliage. Leaves come down, bits of twig, tasselled chestnuts, bouncing from branch to branch, pincushioning a naked toe with fine needles, or falling clear from the bough to plop among the high grass. The autumn clouds slide over the tree-tops and induce a gentle vertigo. The last danglers are in the very crown of the tree — tenacious, inaccessible, defiant. Sweat blurs the aim. The men leave them to bob in the wind and shin down to help the women and children gather the fruit into sacks. In the grass they search for them, in the crannies of the roots, among the bushes; they pick them out with tongs — a twig bent but not broken. Sackful upon sackful builds a green, spiny heap. Then they sit round, wrap sacking over their hands, and split the kernels with a sharp twist of the wrist. The fruit lies in the white womb, burnished, glowing. The husks mount on the one side; on the other, the brown, glistening conkers. For me they had the smell of childhood and the lane behind the house.

Pebbles from My Skull

The wine harvest on these upland farms is quickly over. The grapes in the wooden pails are warm from the sun; they feel like flesh, with a soft female quality like the inside of a thigh. On the top step of the wine cellar there is a long wooden trough with sides a couple of feet deep; it slopes down to a spigot at the lower end. You dip your feet in a pail of cold water and step in.

Your feet sink into the pulp of fruit; feel the resistance of pips and stalks. The juice squirts up between your toes, warm and sticky like blood. You feel the deep satisfaction of the bloomed and tender fruit squelching underfoot. Between times you can lie full out at the end of the sloping trough, draw the spigot, and let the grape juice squirt into your mouth. It is warm, sweet and sticky. Your hands are sticky; your legs are sticky to the knee. The buckets fill quickly and are tipped into the great vats which rise to the ceiling at the back of the cellar, stained with the juice of scores of vintages. After a day or two, if you set your ear to their bellies, you can hear them stir and rumble as if some immense digestive process were under way. The vats are beginning to boil; a scum of impurities rises to the top. From it come clouds of tiny red-headed flies. The air is heady with the fumes of alcohol. The rubbish is skimmed from the top and goes to join the mush of pips, stalks and grapeskins left over from the wine-treading. Squeezed dry in a giant hand-press, the hardened mass of waste is fodder for the swine. The liquid that drains off, mixed with water, is *mezz'vin*, the acidulate drink for the midday break in the fields.

From treading the grapes we ran out one day to watch the bombing of Fidenza. There was a confused rumour in the low clouds, smoke and explosions echoing up into the hills. You can see what rich people they must be, these Americans, said the peasant. They knock things down and don't care.

The Savage Wood

Ploughing is more difficult. The oxen stumble in the clay. Their cloven hooves sink deep and each step is an effort. You must use the goad, oaths, pet-names, objurgations and yells of rage. If the storm slackens the oxen cease to pull. Sometimes you are at the tail of the plough leaning on the handles to make the share bite; sometimes at the beasts' heads tugging at horn or nose-ring, turning them at the end of the rig, with your own feet slipping and sliding in the mire. The oxen pause and blow huge puffs of steam, like mild dragons. Across the valley a long, blasphemous formula echoes to and fro as another team is driven on. At midday the women come into the fields with a basket of hot, baked dough — a kind of *pizza* — wrapped in a cloth, a piece of cheese, and a bottle of thin wine.

To dig a field is more difficult still. Up on the high farms the fields are too steep for the plough. You break them from pasture with the hoe — a giant adze with a blade a foot long. Work starts early. The sun can be long in getting into the little valleys and you shiver as you walk to the foot of the slope. You look up, measuring the field. It seems improbable that two or three pairs of hands will ever turn that stretch of turf. The first blow tells you what the day will be like. If the blade comes out clean, the soil is light and the line of broken clods will move steadily uphill; if it comes out thick with clay, you will have to stop every other stroke and scrape the blade. And so on, all day for eight hours, until the sun sets and the women call from the house. Over supper the men nod and drowse. When the meal is over they push back the plates, lay their heads on their arms and sleep. They rouse themselves for a last look at the oxen. At four they must rise again to feed and water the beasts. On the upland farms the families are small. Procreation requires a margin of energy.

These were share-croppers, *mezzadri*, paying to the landlord half of all they earned — half their eggs, half their cheese, half their milk and half their crops. The main figure in their lives was not the landowner, *il padrone*, but his agent, *il fattore*. The Scottish 'factor'. He lived in the big steading of the *fattoria* and exacted the landlord's due. Next to him came the *guardiano*, the keeper, who preserved the shooting and the woodlands — a man hated by all. We lived in houses where the meal after a long day in the fields was sometimes a platter of hard bread on which the housewife poured a thin purée of tomatoes and a drop of oil. We drank wine without body, which bit like pepper on the tongue. On weekdays we worked in the fields. On Sundays we shaved or had our hair cut and in the dark evenings talked.

Are you Catholics?
No.
Do you believe in God?
No.
Do you hear that, Maria? Educated men and they don't believe in God.
Maybe that's their custom.
I always told you there was no God. Why don't the Allies bomb the Vatican?
A pause.
Why should they?
They'd get rid of the priests. They won't have another chance like this.
Or again:
Where do you come from?
England.
Is that near here?
It's a long way.
Near Africa then?
No — not near Africa.
But you said you came from Africa.
Yes — we were fighting there.
Why do people fight in Africa? They're always fighting there.
Or again:
You should have seen our pots and pans before the Duce took them to make shells. All copper.
And my wedding ring. I had to give it for the war in

The Savage Wood

Abyssinia. Where is Abyssinia?
In Africa.
Mamma mia, always Africa. Are they Christians in Africa?
In Abyssinia — yes.
How do you know?
I've been there.
Fighting?
Yes.
The Abyssinians?
No — the Italians.
Why the Italians?
Because we were at war.
There shouldn't be any wars.

Or again:
In England you eat five times a day.
Who said so?
The Duce.
Well, it's not true.
Do you hear Maria, I always said he told us a pack of lies.
But you sell your wives.
No, but we can divorce them. (Which of Mussolini's propagandists, I wondered, had read *The Mayor of Casterbridge*.)
Ah, that's what we need — divorce. Do you hear, Maria, divorce. But the bloody priests won't let us.

Sometimes I read to them — anything, a schoolbook with insipid fairy-tales or an almanac with riddling saws and equivocal prophecies. They sat and listened. When I stopped they said: 'Read some more. It must be nice to be able to read.'

Paolo had a farm in the foothills above Parma. Parma the Red, he called it. After the last war, he said, the people of Parma were Bolsheviks and took over the factories. But the Bishop called in the army and they had to surrender. There would be more Bolsheviks after this war. And quite right, too. We sat round the table drinking till far into the

Pebbles from My Skull

afternoon. His wine pricked the tongue. At last he got up and we shouldered our hoes. His little boy shuttled to and fro to the cellar, filling the wine bottle, set at the end of the row. Towards evening his wife came running from the house. A German patrol at the road-end. We laid down our hoes and shook hands. Paolo burst into tears. Weeping he followed us to the edge of the wood, glass in one hand, bottle in the other. You must drink it up, he said and wept. We came back after dark to sleep in the hayloft; next morning we woke early. Paolo was in the kitchen with a couple of bottles of wine. It was about five and the light not yet breaking. We drank a bottle each and bade farewell tearfully. The stars were very bright and unsteady. We set out over the crest and cut across a field, stumbling in the ploughland. For an age we groped in circles among the furrows, weak with laughter. We sat down under a hedge and waited for our heads to clear. When we were more sober we crossed the ridge, found a barn and slept it off under the straw.

From village to village and from valley to valley the dialect changed, but basically it kept its nasals and its modified 'u'. *Fueg'*, they said and meant *fuoco*: fire. *Vin*, they said, with a long 'i' and a nasal: wine. Trousers were *braghe* — breeks. I remembered that this was once Cisalpine Gaul.

More than their language I learned their way of thinking and of living. I did not know how hard life could be until I heard an old man cry to children teasing him with the threat of living to a century: 'But I don't want to live, I want to die.' I did not know that life could be restricted to one spot, that one's bridal bed could be one's deathbed, that the days could be tied to a cycle of labour, and life mean, squalid, hard. I learned why the peasants spoil their children, refusing them no liberty; at twelve they are drawn into the struggle. I watched the sudden furies of a woman, beautiful and dirty, with her long hair about her face, as she flung the hoe from her and cursed the fields, the landlord, and the hour of her creation. She had been married on tolerance, bringing with her an illegitimate daughter of ten, an

The Savage Wood

astonishing child with blue eyes and an oval face. The mother paid for her conception daily.

I learned what to eat and how much, and that in a plate of rabbit meat the biggest looking portion is probably the head. (This Ted forgot and re-discovered with oaths.) I learned that the man of the house must make the polenta, sifting a fist-full of maize flour into the boiling pot. When the porridge thickens he must use two hands on the stick. Great bubbles form on the surface and burst again with a sigh. He lifts the pot from the hook over the hearth, puts one hand under it and pours the polenta on to the board. The wife cuts it into slices. Holding one end in her teeth, she runs a thread under the stiffening yellow lava and draws it to her. The thread comes clean through and a slab of polenta falls away. I learned to drink coffee of toasted oats and to suck the boiled feet of a rooster.

We got to know their pleasures — wine, tobacco, the Sunday knowledge that there is nothing more to do than walk over to the village, to sit in the sun away from the wind, to watch the young people dancing to the harmonica, or the old men at their cards, spinning them on to the table with a flick of the wrist or banging them down under a great, horny thumb. Strange suits they have with cups and batons for emblems like a debased Tarot pack.

We found that their enemy was authority — the landlord and his factor, the state and its inspectors, the Duce and the Pope. For them Fascism meant authority. Fascism took their wheat for the communal grain pool, their copper pots for the driving bands of shells, their sons for the wars. It gave them nothing in return. Its enemies, in simple logic, must be their friends.

3

We stepped out into the landscape of the plain on 9 September 1943. Eight weeks — fifty-six days — later, we were still on the wrong side of the Apennines. Sometimes we saw a reconnaissance plane, alone, high up; once, a silver flock of bombers, spinning their condensation trails across the mountains. The peasants brought us little strips of tinfoil. The Anglo-Americans had dropped them. Were they dangerous? We looked at the spiralling metal, Christmas-tree tinsel, and wondered what it might be. We were even more cut off than in the camps; there we had had papers, letters, links with the world. In the high Apennines there were no papers, no radios, only rumour. Mussolini was in Germany. Mussolini was in the North. Mussolini had set up a Republic. The Allies had bombed Rome. They wanted to kill the Pope. There were thousands of partisans in the hills above La Spezia. At the word 'partisan' I felt a warm rush of political romanticism. The Italians were proving again that when a people feel a cause to be their own, they will fight for it. Ted was sceptical. We talked over the situation in a farmyard one Sunday morning. The Allies would soon move. They must before the winter set in. If they didn't, we would try to find the partisans. In the yard a white turkey-cock puffed itself up into scarlet tumescence and flitted its wings in the dust. Then slowly, deliberately, it strutted forward to tread its mate.

Perhaps we stayed so long in this crude Arcadia because we were still not ready to face the world. Yet we had strong reasons for action: Ted as a regular whose career found in war its reason and consummation; both of us as ex-prisoners who had to prove to ourselves that we had not

The Savage Wood

failed by the act of surrender. We talked about it still, but less obsessively than we had, each in our own group, in our prison camps, analysing, speculating, excusing, wondering. Ted certainly had nothing to reproach himself with. In a 'box' forward of Alamein, he and his men had bought time for the line to form. A burst of machine-gun fire killed the anti-tank gunners. He manned their six-pounder, watched the tanks come on in the ranger-finder, and felt the gun leap under him as it fired. They came on still, grinding in the sides of the fox holes, pulping the dead and wounded. He emerged alive.

I, for my part, puzzled over a distributor arm lost in the sand, fallen from my pocket — I supposed — as I lay with my driver in a patch of camel thorn and watched the armoured cars round up the stragglers, the last scurrying trucks. Derelicts, burnt-out tanks, wrecked guns, were dotted like flies over the sand. The sun leapt up and struck. The long flat reaches of the desert rippled in the heat. There was no shade among the camel thorn. My driver had the rosy face of a boy from a new draft, fresh from home. Night came and the sand cooled. We walked over to our truck. I felt in my pocket. The distributor arm was gone. For three days we walked through German columns, Italian encampments, and edged our way round airfields. A sandstorm blew up and dropped as suddenly. It left us in the midst of a group of Italians. Swollen-tongued, I could not answer when they said, with a strange kind of embarrassment: *Che brutto tempo fa*. These were arguments we had gone over a thousand times, to prove that we had the right to be alive when others died. Yet now that we were free we were content to take things easily and feel the edge of danger by degrees.

At least we were fit; no peasant could challenge us with the hoe and beat us. Our fame spread from farm to farm. Could we come for a couple of days? Could we help with the last field? So we hoboed our way across the slopes of the Apennines and saw below us the autumn plain of the north paling towards winter. Sometimes we were impatient and

Pebbles from My Skull

moved across country for a couple of days together; we took turns to be pathfinder. Standing in the farmyard in the early light we would look over the hills and pick a target for the day's march. At a fork in the path the leader chose right or left without explanation; the other followed without question. As night began to fall it became the custom for me to lead. I would pick a farmhouse and make for it through the dusk. Sometimes I baulked at the last minute and turned aside, choosing another house because of a vague presentiment, a hunch, a fear I could neither express nor explain. Ted grumbled a little then swung his sack on to his shoulder and followed on. At the door it fell to me to knock and walk into the lamplight. Ted watched and listened. He had the knack of uttering strange, taciturn growls with an Italian ring to them. When we were in and by the fire we gradually revealed ourselves; they would not turn us away. In the hay we slept close together and woke together. War had taught us to take each day as it came, to eat and sleep and shut our minds against the future.

If our progress was slow we could plead that the terrain did not help us. The northern slopes of the Apennines are bare and eroded. Ridges like the fingers of a bony hand run up into spines and watersheds. The hills are riven by torrents and breached by four rivers: the Taro, the Parma, the Enza and the Secchia. We waded all four.

The Taro was the worst. It has two arms; both were in spate. We crossed one, groping for a foothold among the boulders. Under the opaque, brown water we felt them shift beneath our feet and roll downstream before the impulse of the flood. At each pace our feet, searching for a hold, wavered in the tug of the current. At last the level began to drop to our waists, our knees, our ankles. We spent the night with a peasant on the high spit of land above the confluence of the waters. He received us with surprise; a horse and gig had been swept away that day, trying to pass the ford. In the morning, in our damp clothes, our boots hard from the water, we came down to the main arm: a double channel with a dry bed of boulders in the midst. We

The Savage Wood

each had a stick to wedge in the bed of the river. The first channel was easy — no deeper than the day before; leaning on our sticks we stemmed the rush of the water. We rested on the boulders in midstream and looked across to the far bank. We could see the road running along under the hillside, following the river. Upstream was the railway bridge — guarded, the peasants said; downstream, the road-bridge at Fornovo di Taro. Suddenly we were aware of the lunacy of our situation — sitting in the midst of a flooded river in full view of the main road. There is in war and danger generally an element of farce. We sat on the boulders, while the water streamed out of our boots and down our trouser legs, and laughed.

The second channel was stronger and deeper. The boulders shifted as they took our weight. The water broke in a wave against our sides and met again below us in a whirling vortex. Our sticks struggled in our hands, swept downstream and up to the surface by the force of the current. With each step the river bed shelves by inches. At the deepest point the water was up to our armpits. It made you catch your breath and shiver. Under the road on the far bank we emptied our boots and struck up over the hillside.

Hilaire Belloc, rollicking along the Path to Rome, was carried over at this very spot on the shoulders of a peasant. It was, he says 'as cold as Acheron, the river of the dead'. In the rush of the water the two men fell, then 'it was easy to understand how the Taro can drown men, and why the peasants dreaded those little ribbons of water'. He paid his Christopher three lire.

One morning in late October — there was frost on the ground — we saw across a spur a grey castle on a hilltop. Canossa, said a peasant, a very old castle. I thought of the Emperor standing barefoot for three days in the snow at its gates begging for absolution, of winter and the cold of the peaks. A week later we woke in a hard frost and saw that the

Pebbles from My Skull

Apennines had whitened overnight. We must get over before the cols were blocked. That day we left cross-country paths and took courage to walk on the highway. We came on to it by a bridge — the road from Modena to the pass of the Abetone and the frontier with Tuscany. We walked on against a snell wind. On a serpentine of curves we passed a flock of sheep and called a greeting to the herdsman. We walked through villages and past wayside inns. Townspeople, evacuees, strolling on the country road like migrants out of season, turned and stared at us as we marched past. The Apennines rose white-tipped before us. A day's walk from the pass we spent a night in a house by the roadside — rich peasants with a nephew evacuated from the cities of the plain, a college boy who showed off for our benefit. The road was very quiet, we said — no traffic. They laughed. The pass was blocked.

Next morning there was a flurry of snow along the road. Soon the trees and the roadside grass were flecked with patches of white. We were high up now above the chestnuts and the scrub oaks and into the conifers. The snow lay in little drifts which stirred and twitched when a gust of wind came down from the head of the glen. Across the valley we could see the snow-line drawn across the hillside; we were well above it. The wind cut through our shirts and nipped the breath in our throats. The snow became deep and unbroken. Like oxen in the mud, we pulled each step out of the drifts. The road levelled to the pass and then began to dip. I looked down and saw that on the southern slope the snow thinned quickly. Ted was shivering and faltering in his stride. There was an inn by the roadside below the snow-line, half a mile on. I pushed ahead. The snow flaked from my boots on the bare mountain road. I thought of the warmth of the inn. There was a hum of voices. I pushed at the door and found myself in a roomful of Fascist militia. They looked at me with mild interest. I greeted them and glanced round as if expecting someone to step forward and welcome me to the warmth. No one stirred. I shook my head as if to say: He isn't there. They turned back to their

The Savage Wood

talk. I walked out again. The door fell to behind me and the din of voices was muted. Outside I met Ted, recovering now and able to go on. We walked steadily, checking the impulse to glance back. There were no shouts, no running steps, no hue and cry. A mile or so on we stopped at a shepherd's hut tucked away under the brink of the road. He had a wife with a pale, calm face. They spoke Tuscan. Tomorrow will be better, I said. We slept with the sheep and goats in a bed of chestnut leaves, in a low hut, stinking of droppings and urine. But it was warm with their breath and the heat of their packed bodies.

Standing on the edge of the valley we looked next day clear across bright sunny country to the marble mountains of Carrara; their peaks gleamed like snow. The land fell steeply below us into a deep valley, full of tracks and streams, with good cover. We ran scuffling down. The bushes caught the air and the sun was warm.

It was the first week in November. The Allies were somewhere above Naples — three hundred miles to the south.

Looking for the cottage twenty years later, I failed to find it. The whole picture of the mountain pass, as I have it in mind, is at variance with facts of geography. I remember a long valley on our right; it is on the left. The pass over the col is longer than I remember it. The inn is not where I thought it to be. My topography is more real.

4

We crossed into Tuscany on 10 November. The feast of St Martin — it falls on the 12th — we spent in a cottage on the edge of the chestnut forest. From the door we looked across the intricate, folded valleys of the Garfagnana. This was true Romantic landscape of forest, mountain, hilltop villages, castles on abrupt precipices. It was shadowy, accidented, soft in colouring, 'horrid' in detail. There were three girls in the house — in their teens or early twenties. They had made a cake. We sat round the fire at night and ate it, drinking *vin santo*, sweet wine made from dried grapes and kept for holidays. The girls were pretty and flirtatious, conscious of themselves, dressed to please and safe in the knowledge that next day we would move on. I listened to the cadence of their speech and felt that we had crossed into a land where life had greater ease, promised more than mere labour.

Next day we moved off along the mule track. Above us great sharp ridges ran up to the snowy peaks of the Abetone. The path doubled to and fro, falling hundreds of feet to a torrent, yellowy-white with snow-water, then climbing again to traverse the opposite wall of the ravine. At the top there might be a clearing, a plateau high up among the chestnuts with a single stone hut. A mule clattered its hooves in the stall. In the loneliest of these we found a charcoal-burner — a widower with two children. The girl kept house. The son worked with his father, jogging on the wooden pack-saddle up the rain-channelled paths, through the bedraggled woods, to clearings where wood smouldered to charcoal beneath a cone of divots. Together they packed charcoal into the sacks till they

The Savage Wood

bulged tight. A criss-cross of supple twigs, quickly interlaced, sealed the mouth. Then they turned down again to the hut. The mule picked its way before them through the thick, slippery drifts of chestnut leaves.

There was about the family a sense of warmth and comradeship which embraced even strangers like ourselves. At night we roasted chestnuts in a long-handled frying pan and drank the thin wine of the hills. The rain dripped and sizzled in the hearth. The man sat by the fireside and listened as Ted and I spoke together.

'You are from Scotland, aren't you?' he asked suddenly with a pure Glasgow accent. The girl stopped her housework and smiled proudly as her father told how, like others from the hills, as a young man, he had travelled north through France to the Clydeside, there to huckster plaster Madonnas to the devout Irish of the industrial slums. Having sold his wares he had gone into the pits. The depression of the thirties had driven him home to the forest.

His daughter was mixing a paste of coarse, pinkish flour. I dipped my finger in the bowl; the paste was sweet with a bitter tang at the back of it. Chestnut flour. She lifted a huge pair of tongs from the chimney-side and warmed them in the flame. Each arm ended in a circular plate — a diminutive girdle. On each she dropped a little oil; it hissed and smoked on the hot metal. Then she added a blob of paste, closed the tongs firmly and thrust them back into the heat. When she drew them out it was to release a hot, thin pancake into our hands. We ate them with creamy cheese. I remembered an old woman in Breughel's Lenten market-place, bending over a fire of sticks with her bowl of batter at her side and her long-handled tongs.

We slept in the hay above the mule. It clattered in its stall all night. The spot was Pian della Fava, near the village of Antelminelli, in the Province of Lucca.

By early December we had come wandering among the hills to above Pistoia. From our map of Italy we knew we had a main line to cross with a river this side of it. These were days of rain and sleet, with the paths squelching under

Pebbles from My Skull

foot and the trees dripping above. I remember a fire in a cave where we dried our clothes at midday and coming out were caught in snow and rain that soaked us to the skin once more. I remember a priest of little charity who turned us away and a poor woman who took us in and made a great pot of *gnocchi*, potato dumplings with a sauce of oil and tomatoes. I remember coming out on to the bare uplands beyond the tree-line and eating bread and cheese in a stone sheepfold. The next valley held the river and railroad. Beyond it we would see Florence. We decided to stop for the night and reconnoitre our passage.

There were one or two scattered lights on the hillside. We dropped down past a lonely farmhouse and found, below us, strung along the hillside, a scattered village of a thousand souls. A village could mean authorities, a Fascist post perhaps, *carabinieri*. So in the twilight we struck uphill again. At the turning of a narrow path a man came towards us — medium height, sideburns, a fringe of moustache on his lip, a hat on the back of his head and a raincoat, like a gunman out of an Irish play. He had his right hand in his coat pocket.

I greeted him and made to pass on. He blocked the way. Ted walked with a stout ash-plant in his hand. He raised it on to his shoulder and gripped it with both hands.

The stranger stepped back a little and smiled. We were wearing British issue boots, he said. We agreed in a challenging way and asked if it was any business of his what we wore. He asked if we had heard of the partisans. We told him we were sceptical. He grinned and said we were lucky because he was a liaison officer with a partisan formation. If we didn't believe him we could come into the village. There were more like us there. We looked at each other and debated. You're afraid, he said, and I don't blame you. I'll go on ahead, if you like. Ted said we should chance it. We stood aside to let him pass, slung our sacks over our shoulders and walked on through the dusk. He stopped and turned round.

'What's your name?'

The Savage Wood

I told him.

'Too difficult. I'll call you Carlino. And the other? Edoardo. Fine.'

So I took a new name.

At the edge of the village we stopped at a house-door. Our guide knocked and walked straight in. A tall fair man was washing at the sink. He turned and spoke to us in the accents of Yorkshire.

We slept the night on a mattress in the upper floor of a long, rambling house. There was nothing else in the room except bags of seed, onions, shallots, gaudy heads of maize, apples and pears wizening in a corner. We woke and looked out into a bowl among the hills. A stream tumbled down by steps and stairs to a mill. Below the mill-race it plunged over the edge of the bowl into a defile. The sides of the bowl were abrupt, thick with chestnuts. High up beyond them there were beeches on the hilltop. Level with our eyes a white road cut along the hillside through the trees, made a sharp angle at a bridge over the stream and doubled towards us into the village. Below us the walls of the defile came to a knife edge, marked with a line of conifers, then dropped abruptly to the river we must cross. Beyond the river, like a vast groyne, a long hill ran down into the Florence plain. It was bare and grey. You had the impression of a solid lump of primeval rock. Between its boulders there seemed to be stunted undergrowth. Ted looked at it with a kind of affectionate recognition. Like the North-West Frontier, he said.

People were stirring in the village. Mules were being saddled. A peasant walked down into the fields with a hoe. We felt strange in the midst of it all, half doubtful, half afraid, inclined to giggle, wondering what would come next. The house was quiet. We pulled on our boots and walked downstairs. There was no one in the kitchen. We put a pan of milk on the charcoal and fanned it. We were eating when our host came in with the same jaunty air as when we met him on the path above the village. He saw from the way we turned that we were tense and on the defensive. He laughed and slapped us on the shoulder. We

Pebbles from My Skull

were scared last night, weren't we? he said. All dressed up but wearing British army boots. The memory convulsed him. Suddenly he became serious and began to talk. If we really wanted to join the partisans he could get us across to them. Where? we asked. He pointed out of the window. Do you see the long ridge, he said, that's the Calvana, the bare mountain. The 'c' he aspirated Tuscan fashion. Now beyond it, do you see another mountain? The peak was powdered with snow. We could see a bluff wooded shoulder and a bare sweep of alp. That's Monte Morello, he said. That's where they are. But you'll have to wait a couple of weeks till I can arrange things.

The door opened and a small, sturdy girl in her twenties came in. She had a clear complexion, fine features and an odd sad look. He went over to her, put his arm round her. It was a gesture we had not seen between any peasant and his wife. This is Carlino, he said, and this is Edoardo. This is Gina, my wife. You can trust her. We're going for a walk, he added. I'm taking them up the hill to Le Valli. It's an empty farmhouse he said. I was born there. My father was a peasant.

We felt strangely exposed walking through the village street. A man passed with a donkey. He greeted our guide. We saw the quick glance with which he took us in. Women drawing water at the conduit laid down their pitchers and looked at us quietly. We turned a corner. A man was walking towards us in the dark green uniform of the militia; his carbine was slung. We both turned and bolted with a clatter of boots on the cobbles. Suddenly we stopped. We could hear our guide laughing and walking back towards us. He had his arm round the militiaman's waist. We stopped and let them come up. The militiaman shuffled along with an embarrassed grin on his face. This is Dante, said our guide, he's not a bad chap — a bit fond of the bottle — guards the railway line. Have you got your hand-grenades? he asked, thrusting his hand into the militiaman's knapsack. That's good — we might need them some day. *Ciao*, Dante, *ciao*, he said. The militiaman gave some sort of

The Savage Wood

greeting, bowed his head and went trotting off down into the valley.

Above the village we clambered up to a lonely steading. It stood on the edge of the woods. A couple of steps and you were lost in a tangle of broom and scrub oak. Le Valli. Here thirty-five years before he had been born, the son of a poor peasant. His name was Franco. As a boy he had known the harsh discipline of work in the fields and hated it. When his father died he decided to leave the land. The alternative lay in the valley where the wool-mills line and straddle the river all the way down to Prato and the plain. There he picked and unpicked old rags for the cloth merchants to re-spin into coarse suitings for market booths. The machines were without guards; the air, full of dust and fibre. His chest was affected. He came back to the village making a living as he could, doing odd jobs, determined to be free. Each morning the workers clattered down the hillside to the mills; under Mussolini's autarchy industry flourished. But the mill hands remembered 1918 and the workers' councils, how they seized power in the valley, and how in the twenties the Fascists took their revenge. Franco, for his part, remembered his father dosed with castor oil and tied in a sack, like a calf ready for the market, to lie in his own filth and weakness. He knew that Fascism degrades and by degrading its victim finds justification for murder. So he sat in the hills and waited.

What I found difficult to understand in him was that he was not *un pur*. He was spendthrift with a hint of the spiv and a spiv's love of little conspiracies. At times there was in his behaviour something equivocal, which I found slightly frightening. As for the villagers they both feared and admired him. For the young men from the mills he was a leader, a man who forced them to think, urged them to discontent, mocked at their fears. The old looked on him with suspicion. His clear and open aim was to destroy life as they knew it — to break the bond that held the peasant to the soil and to the landlord, to liberate the women from superstition, drudgery, the tight, merciless circle of their

45

Pebbles from My Skull

lives. His wife was a peasant girl and did the peasant chores. But he helped her, insisted that she dress decently, showed her affection, comforted her for her barrenness. The other women said she gave herself airs; he protected her both for her own sake and as a symbol of an essential human liberty. He was a strange man, strangely compounded, utterly brave.

5

It is not difficult to cross a river-line, even with a road before it and a railway beyond, guards on the tunnels and patrols along the track. Luck, a moonless night, and a guide will do it. It is more difficult to step voluntarily into danger. Up to now we had been unarmed fugitives, subject always to treachery and recapture; liable, in the worst of cases, to be obscurely shot. But our luck had held. We had turned thoughtlessly into a village street with our sacks on our backs to find a *carabiniere* patrol a few paces away. In dark and mist we had trudged uphill past a German fatigue party carrying blankets to some bivouac on a mountain road. In each case we had got away with it, restraining the impulse to run until they were out of sight. Now we had to decide whether to accept the hazards of the *franctireur*.

We had a couple of weeks to make up our minds. We spent them in the empty farmhouse above the village, waiting for a message from Franco. There was a constant rustling of mice in the attic, where crab-apples, sorb-apples, pears, and a few cobwebbed grapes, were laid out on the floor. By day the women, passing on their way to gather firewood, called in with a bowl of pasta or a dish of beans. We ate ravenously. The women wept over us and cursed the war. At night we dropped down into the village and supped at their tables. They were braver than their men, warm, generous, tough and curiously reckless. They know us up here, they said, they won't dare come. We doubted it and slept deep down in the straw in a little cave by the wall. We woke one night to hear the wooden bolt drawn softly back. There was a sound of breathing and a gentle groping noise as something — a long stick, a hay-fork — was pushed deep

Pebbles from My Skull

into the straw, probing and searching. When at last the door closed we heard a faint scurry of feet recede along the stony path.

From that night on we slept in the hills, continually on the move from one shelter to another. One long day we lay in a little stone hut among dripping brushwood and heard search-parties comb the woods. The crack of hand-grenades echoed through the wet valley. There was an occasional burst of fire. At night a boy came through the undergrowth and led us to warmth and shelter. It was a small stone building like a windowless cottage. A huge log fire blazed in the middle of the stone floor; flames and sparks shot up to the ceiling. Smoke filled the room and hung a couple of feet from the floor. Every now and then the boy or his father got up from lying by the fire and climbed a ladder into the loft. You could hear him move about on the rough hewn rafters, dowsing a red spot where the wood had begun to smoulder and turning the sweet chestnuts, spread to dry on the canes, that made a ceiling between the beams. In a week or ten days a mule would bring a little petrol-driven mill up from the valley to grind them into sweet flour. Meanwhile we tended the fire, roasted chestnuts, drank red wine, talked.

Here one day an English major found us. He had his batman with him. He said we were under his command. We did not get up from the fire. We didn't think much of senior officers, we explained, and preferred to be on our own. He went away stooping, blonde, wet and dispirited, unmistakably an English officer. Two days later he was taken by a militia patrol and led down the village street with his hands pinioned behind him. We heard the news with a mixture of guilt and satisfaction. We had seen our elders bungle their trade of war, surrender, and then in the camps use their rank to obtain privilege, jumping — or trying to jump — the hungry queues. We were still bitter.

The night after his capture, for safety's sake, we spent in a badger's den — a narrow tunnel, screened with brushwood, slanting down into a steep hillside. We slid in feet first. The

The Savage Wood

rocky walls pinned our arms to our sides. Rain trickled from the mouth of the hole in a little stream and slowly, icily, ran down the front of my shirt. In a fit of claustrophobia Ted cursed me until I agreed to wriggle out into the dark. We walked blindly through driving rain until we stumbled into a deserted hut with a broken roof and a muddy floor. In one corner there was a glow of ashes. We dozed, standing against the wall, with our heads leaning on our arms and the warmth of the ash rising to our faces. We were impatient to cross the river-line.

In part we chose to cross for quite practical reasons. We felt a net of danger tightening round us. We wanted arms to defend ourselves. We guessed that movement would be increasingly difficult now that the snows were spreading. We wanted a secure base for the winter. With luck the partisans would give us both.

Beyond that there were, in my case certainly, reasons unspoken and not entirely clear even to myself. I was suffering still from the deep trauma of capture and the fear that I had somehow been lacking in a moment of test. Behind that again, shamefully tucked away, was the greater guilt that I had been content not to fight in Spain. Across the river and the bare mountain on the peak we saw each day, dark with woods and patched with bare grassy meadows, were men who would give me the chance to prove myself.

Before we left we came down into the village again. They had made a hide for us in a brushwood-store. One bale of wood came out to show a narrow tunnel. We crawled through it into the darkness and sat on a layer of some soft, fragrant substance — the refuse from the chestnut mill. For two days and nights we lived in the dark and strove to drive past the reluctant hours. Sleep became a burden, a stupefying escape from consciousness, from which we were wakened by the mice squeaking round our food. We slung it from the roof and lay down again. We had lost track of night and day. At last someone unplugged the tunnel and we emerged. It was dark and moonless. We ate supper at a peasant house halfway down to the valley and waited for

Pebbles from My Skull

Franco. He came in with his jaunty air wearing the same raincoat as when first we met.

'I have brought Gina,' he said, and his wife followed him in at the door, greeted us with a quiet smile.

We had a dozen miles to walk over the hills. But first we must pass the road, the river and the railway.

The path ran steeply down with a rush of water beside it. The night was cold and absolutely quiet. Our boots rang out on the path. Looking up we could see against the dark of the sky the deeper black of the hillsides. There were a few stars between the clouds. The path began to widen. We could hear the river ahead. A white strip was the main road. We walked along it to the last house in a file of workers' cottages. We were no longer on our own but were being drawn into a web whose centre lay in Florence with the Committee of National Liberation. There was a youth inside with another man, who seemed to be his father. We shook hands. The young man led us down to the riverside and we waded across. Gina gasped at the coldness of the water. On the other side the young man left us. Before us a long stretch of grass and stone ran up, roofing the tunnel. After an hour's climb on the naked hillside we stopped on the crest. We could see the Calvana running away on either side of us, bare and rocky.

On the far side we rested. The stars had come out. Across a wide valley stood our mountain, a dark volcanic peak. Gina was cold and Franco in a wild moment set a match to a bush. It flared like a signal fire. He exclaimed with pleasure and set light to another, holding his hands to the heat and laughing.

'I bet the militia wonder what's going on,' he said, 'I bet they are shitting themselves.' He was a man who held his enemies and all danger in contempt.

The fire died and we walked on into an open valley. Just before dawn we had crossed it and were on the shoulder of the mountain. The path climbed up to a church set on a little crest, crossed the crest and forked. We took the upper path. Half a mile on was a cattle-shed set back into the hill. A

The Savage Wood

couple of hundred yards away was a poor upland farm. Below the land fell away in a narrow valley to the village of Morello and beyond, on the edge of the plain, to the proletarian township of Sesto Fiorentino. The plain of the Arno was vague and misty; on the far side was a low range of hills. Beyond them was Pisa and the sea.

'Sesto', says Baedeker's Northern Italy *(1889 edition), 'is the best starting-point for an ascent of Monte Morello (3,065 ft). We go via Doccia (1½ hr), la Collina, whence we proceed to the left, via Morello, to (25 min.) S Giusto a Gualdo, where the easier of the two paths to the summit diverges beyond the church. Passing (10 min.) a cattle-shed (to the left), we soon reach the south-east peak, La Casaccia (3,020 ft) which commands an extensive view.' Baedeker's cattle-shed was our headquarters.*

I don't know what I had expected — certainly not a couple of sleepy boys with straw still clinging to their jackets, newly risen from their beds in the back of a cattle-shed. We shook hands and began to talk, looking for points of contact, trying to break the ice. They addressed me with the formal third person *Lei*. I remonstrated with them. Well, they said, we don't know you well enough to say *tu* and only the Fascists use *voi*. Where were the others? They replied using nicknames, *noms de guerre* — Baffo, Lo Slavo, Salt'alla Macchia, i Russi, Totò. Baffo had gone down to spend the night with his family in Sesto. Il Capo, the boss, was in Florence. The Russians were foraging over the hills. So were the Yugoslavs. Totò was out hunting. He came back half an hour later — a tiny, wizened man with exophthalmic eyes, a shot-gun in his hand, a bandolier slung over his shoulder. At his belt dangled a goldfinch and a couple of thrushes. In a hungry country there are no bird-watchers. Then Franco left with Gina and we were alone.

It was an idle, pointless morning. The diffidence between

Pebbles from My Skull

us was slow to thaw. Why were the Anglo-Americans so long in coming? Why did the bombers aim so badly? Why did Radio Londra tell the partisans to go home? Slowly they began to reassemble. First the Yugoslavs — Tommaso, a rosy-faced peasant boy with a hundredweight of potatoes slung over one shoulder: Mirko, a student from Zagreb, thin, fair, sharp-faced. In him I first met the revolutionary fervour of the Slavs. Towards evening, the two Russians, laughing together. They poured out from their sacks bread, sheep's-milk cheese, salami. From the priest across the mountain. The elder of them shivered. A sergeant-major from a collective farm in the Ukraine, he was shaken from time to time with a malarial ague. He had a thin, worn face. He did not expect to see his home again. The other, Andrey, a prolet, an industrial worker from Moscow, stocky, thick-set, with a broad flat face, like an extra from a Soviet film. His worker's cap, worn straight over the eyes, was all part of the role. Lieutenant in an artillery regiment, he had been taken at Stalingrad. He was confident, defiant, distant, and without fear. We spoke Russian together. These are not real Communists, he said, they're just playing. Last of all, Baffo with a fair moustache from which he took his name, a bank clerk from Sesto, plump, always clowning and laughing.

In the summer of 1960, driving along the strada panoramica *cut into the flank of Morello, we came in the evening to the end of the asphalt. The Sunday couples had parked their cars on the terrace and stood on the edge to look down on Florence. A small boy touted wild flowers. In the bar at the limit of the asphalt they said there was a partisan monument along the cart track and past the Fonte della Serpe, with its healing waters. At the Well of the Serpent two men drank, half believing, half sceptical. On the downward slope there were young conifers, ten feet high or more. I remembered that they had been mere seedlings in 1943. A pair of lovers lay on the grass behind a dyke; so close they had blotted out the world. A patch of paint on a stone told us to turn off into the pine wood. A peasant plunged about among the trees, rounding up his cattle. The*

The Savage Wood

monument was an ugly pillar of local stone. The wreaths were torn, withered, tawdry with red ribbon. Pious litter. In the list of the dead, killed by the Germans near this spot in August 1944, was Baffo's name.

At dusk we went down to the farmhouse. We cooked from our own stores. I felt for the first time the ambiguous mood of the peasantry. Fear alternated in their minds with detestation of the regime. They knew that, in the last resort, the partisans could clear out. They themselves were bound to their steading and to the cycle of the year, with olives to be picked far down on the hillside, the pig to be slaughtered and cured, fodder to be cut for the oxen in the byre.

We slept that night in the stone cattle-shed. There was no sentry. Rising after midnight I looked out and saw Orion overhead. A clear frosty night. When I lay down again I felt in the straw for my short Italian carbine. It was my twenty-eighth birthday.

Next day we dug our armoury out of the straw and checked it over. There was a heavy machine-gun, water-cooled, the classic weapon of revolution. Ted taught me elementary gun drill. To him it meant not the Winter Palace and the wars of intervention but the little stone forts, the *sangars*, of the Frontier wars. I sat behind the gun and pressed the trigger with my thumbs. The sights were set at 1,000 metres. It would have laid a cone of fire along the path up from the valley. I remembered my small-arms instructor asking through his dentures with a Glasgow drawl: What is to 'enfilade'? And the ritual shout from the class: To enfilade is to sweep with fire throughout the whole length *of*. With an accent on the 'of'. Illiterate, he allowed no deviation from the formula.

We asked how much ammunition there was. None. So we buried the gun in the hay again.

There was a Breda light machine-gun, still greasy from the armourer's store, with a box of thin black magazines, all fully loaded. The machine-gunner was our cook, a broad-

Pebbles from My Skull

shouldered Sardinian, with the slight flabbiness of a man who has spent his days over the galley fires, tasting the rations. We argued about the loading of the magazines. They were too full and the springs would suffer. He denied it. He was going to reload with tracer anyway. One in five tracer. But first he wanted to test the gun. Setting it up outside the shed he fired off a whole magazine in a couple of long bursts. The bullets went whining off the rock he had chosen as his mark. The valley filled with sound; the hills flung it down and over the plain. The peasant women came to the door in terror. The Sardinian laughed. Each bullet is a shot seed; the burst of fire is orgasmic. In this sense, war is the sterile self-abuse of lonely men.

There was a Russian automatic rifle without ammunition. Heavy but well made. It was preserved as a political symbol. Andrey took it up, handling it with affection.

There were a few of the long-barrelled Italian army rifles — 1898 model. There were as many short modern Italian carbines with high velocity and a crude sight. There was a rucksack full of the little red Italian hand-grenades. Two thin metal cups; an explosive charge in the larger of the two; in the other a lead ball. They exploded on impact, the ball driving a needle home into a percussion cap set in the charge. Or they might fall on their sides and not explode at all. In Abyssinia I had seen the village children gashed by the duds left over from a mock battle between two platoons of my own company. On the battlefields of Eritrea they slaughtered the baboons scrabbling among the debris and the graves.

For the rest of the day we waited. With Ted I walked over the shoulder of the mountain and saw at our feet, among the haze rising from the Arno, the squat dome of Santa Maria del Fiore and Giotto's campanile. It gave edge to our isolation to think of the morning life of the city, the offices, the shops, trams, fiacres, the dressmakers and the shoemakers, the little workshops and the long factory sheds. It gave us, too, a sudden shock of insecurity to see how close we were to the city, to the barracks, the fortress, police

The Savage Wood

headquarters, the *Ortskommandantur*. Yet the city was our base, from which Il Capo would return any day with money, ammunition, or orders, perhaps, to move off, up in the high mountains above Bologna where the Garibaldi brigades were forming.

That evening he came limping up from Sesto. Lanciotto, one of two brothers, in peace-time a butcher in a village outside Florence. A tall fair-haired man in his thirties, square-faced, handsome in an obvious way, a little vain. He had the broken nose of a professional boxer. His limp was from a wound in the Abyssinian war. It had meant that in this one he had been confined to garrison duties in Florence. On 8 September he had loaded a truck with what weapons he could lay hands on — rifles, machine-guns, ammunition, mortars and mortar bombs, and driven off up the side of Monte Morello. It was from the caches formed that day that our armoury came. He was a fighter, a Communist, innocent of doctrine, fearless himself but with no knack of leading men. His vanity was harmless, something from his boxing days that still clung to him. He said we had to wait.

Christmas passed. We walked down in little groups to the farms nearer the valley with rifles slung on our shoulders. As we went Ted taught me where to site ambushes and explained the elementary strategy of hill-fighting — the feigned retreat over a ridge that makes the enemy below get on his feet and run uphill into concealed fire; the decoy shots that make a column, strung out along a mountain path, turn their backs on the riflemen hidden on the other side of the valley. We stopped at a miller's house. The women were outside washing the linen in the icy water of a mountain stream. At midday we ate pig's blood dusted with flour and fried in oil, a dark spongy mess, like artificial rubber. All afternoon we played *lotto* and recognized in it our own housey-housey. Thirty-one, shouted the caller, the years of our Lord. Later we walked down to the plain and there in Sesto spent the night. Now I first learned that Florence was Red and felt the solidarity of the urban proletariat, heard of the strikes in the Galilei engineering works and of the sealed

Pebbles from My Skull

trains taking human cargoes — political prisoners? Jews? prisoners of war? — up through the valley to Bologna and the north. And, at second-hand, something of the killer squads of the Resistance, the GAP (*Gruppi Azione Partigiani*), founded by Dario, the Tuscan railway worker, who commanded the Garibaldi formations in Emilia. A few months later they were to shoot down, in the streets of Florence, Giovanni Gentile, philosopher and writer, perhaps the only man of intellectual distinction to declare openly for the Fascist Republic. In Rome, on 23 March 1944, they would explode a bomb in the Via Rasella, killing thirty-three South Tyrolean volunteers enrolled in the German military police, inspiring the massacre that same day of three hundred and fifty-five prisoners in the Ardeatine Caves.

We walked off armed through the early morning streets and up into the hills.

In the shed the waiting sparked off tensions. A boy handling his rifle fired a round which smacked into the stone. Disarmed, he wept and promised to be more careful. The Russians looked on, shaking their heads. These were boys of the 1925 class, called up by Mussolini's Social Republic, technically deserters and subject to the pain of death. They were very frightened and hid it by scuffling and bragging. There was a brothel — a good one — near the edge of the city. They wanted to go down '*a donne*'. It was Christmas after all and there wasn't much fun sitting about on the hill. Lanciotto read them a lecture on proletarian morality. They grumbled and subsided.

At midday we ate a local delicacy — calf's bowel. Boiled lengths of white hose-pipe.

In the evening Lanciotto set off again. It was dark early. I divided the night into hour watches and suggested that we share them out. To my surprise they agreed. But in the night they would not rise when called. Only Ted, the Yugoslavs and the Russians stood to their watch. Next morning we argued slightly but they refused to see the point. They won't come, they said, they're too frightened,

The Savage Wood

the 'Repubblicchini'. I found the nickname admirably malicious, a diminutive variant on 'Repubblicani', it summed up the moral squalor of Mussolini's Social Republic.

With Totò I argued politics. He was a mechanic. I had known men like him before in the trade unions and in the Labour Colleges — quick, practical, deeply read in the classics of revolution, but rigid in his thought. An autodidact, he feared to let his mind move into the open. He was, without knowing it, a Trotskyite, a romantic revolutionary, with a deep faith in the *levée en masse* and an equally deep ignorance of the Russian situation. He was a man who had known the inside of the Fascist prisons and the summary justice of the secret tribunals. From him I learned the names of the Italian revolutionaries — Antonio Gramsci, dead in 1936, after ten years of captivity, who had spoken for the workers of Turin in the broad tradition of Rosa Luxembourg, and of new men like Ercole Ercoli who broadcast from Moscow, whose real name, it was whispered, was Togliatti. Totò was a townee, who detested hills and mountain paths; only the fact that he had escaped from prison at the armistice and dared not risk recapture kept him where he was. On fine days he strolled abroad and shot song-birds. So we ate *pasta cogli uccellini*.

At last Lanciotto came back. We were to move off to the high mountains — but in two stages. The main body was to cross over to the Calvana and wait there at a farmhouse in a hollow of the mountain; Totò would take a detail to collect explosives over the back of Morello and rendezvous with us on the bare mountain. Ted was to be of his party. They left that evening.

War is a great school of casualness. Ted went off up the hillside with a See you sometime. He was, in fact, at a turning-point in his life. Our paths had branched. Chance took him to Florence to wait for a guide across the Swiss frontier. Boredom made him chafe at the waiting. Taking a train to Venice he looked in vain for a fishing-

boat to carry him down the Adriatic, put up in a hotel full of German officers, and returned safely to Florence. From Swiss internment he passed back to his battalion on the Italian front. The end of the campaign brought him back to the farm of Toccalmatto and the Tedeschi family. Reaching up to a hiding-place in the wall, behind a fly-spotted photograph, they gave him back his ring.

6

Very early in the morning we broke camp. The heavy machine-gun we left in the straw but we took the Breda. We were laden with provisions, ammunition, and arms. My portion was the machine-gun tripod and its ammunition pack. There was a sleepy confusion before we set off. By dawn we had still a main road and a small river between us and the Calvana. We crossed the road and lay together under the bank as an armoured car went patrolling on its blind way over our heads. At the river they offered to carry me across; it was inconceivable that an officer might wet his feet. The water was barely knee-deep but icily cold. On the far side there were patches of snow. It was a hard, slow climb. In the valley below us we could see the huts of a militia camp, the sentry-towers and figures moving about across the parade ground. That was where the armoured car was based. By midday we had reached the crest of the ridge. There was a cup in the hills; it held a group of houses and, above them, on the slope, a large barn. To reach it you had to come through a gap in the hills; the track lay between high grassy walls. There were a couple of girls tending a flock of sheep and spinning wool on their distaffs. We ate hungrily, sharing our food with the peasants.

In the afternoon we settled down in the barn. It was a long building, set into a steep slope, so that, at the back, the roof ran down almost to the grass of the hillside. There were two doors. One, in the side, faced the steading. When you went in you found a huge stack of hay. If you climbed on top you were level with the second door. Set in the gable, it gave on to a square stone threshing-floor shut in by a low stone wall with a gap in the middle. We set up the Breda to cover the

Pebbles from My Skull

gap and, beyond it, the track through the hills. That night we slept in the warm straw. I had a Russian on either side of me. It was the pattern we had come to adopt. We could talk together.

The weather had set fine and cold. To wash in the morning we had to break the ice in the fountain. With Lanciotto I walked right along the Calvana to a tall iron cross set at its very extremity. Here a contact man would meet us. At our feet was Prato with its road and rail junction. No messenger came, but in his stead Lanciotto's brother, younger and more exuberant, and Lanciotto's blonde wife. We sat in the sun and talked. There was a great noise in the eye of sun. We blinked up and saw the glint of a fuselage. Then down below us the outskirts of the town rocked and burst into clouds of smoke and dust. We watched the formation wheel and turn away. No fighters rose from the airfields. There was not a single burst of anti-aircraft fire in the sky. The planes were four engined, very high and very beautiful. The railway was untouched. It was our first sight of pattern bombing.

On two successive days we walked out along the ridge. No one came. On the third day Andrey got restive. He wanted to kill Fascists, not sit on a hillside. Meanwhile he would visit the priest on the other side of Morello. The sergeant-major went with him: *Ochen'horoshy pop*, he said. A very good priest.

I was sent off to forage. Down in the valley where the railway ran there was a *fattoria* belonging, they said, to a rich Englishman with an unpronounceable name. Lanciotto felt that I, if anyone, should be able to extract something from the *fattore*. With one of the boys of the 1925 class as rifleman to cover me I set out through a grey morning with sudden, swirling showers of snow. I wore a black shepherd's cloak, a black beret, an olive-green Italian army pullover and brown skiing trousers. My cloak streamed behind me in the wind. On the top of the bare mountain the wind was so keen that it hurt my face to look in the teeth of it and see Migliana, Franco's village, across the valley almost level

The Savage Wood

with my eyes. Below us was the river — a thin stream running between stretches of boulders, diverted along its length into lades and conduits to drive the machinery in the mills. As far as the eye could see they succeeded each other, their glass and corrugated roofs blocking the narrow valley. We dropped down between olive groves, through a cluster of houses. We stopped to drink at a fountain. An old man watched us reflectively without speaking.

Years later I found him again standing by his door, an old man in the sun, living in the presence of the ineluctable end. I stopped and asked if he remembered the partisans. Yes, he said, it must be a great satisfaction to you — una gran bella soddisfazione — to come back and see a spot where death was so close.

At last we were at the riverside. There was a foot-bridge and a path. The *fattoria* was the big house before the bridge. I set the boy to watch from a bank above our road and went down, to find nothing but a sour bitch of a woman who refused even a loaf of bread. I walked back but the boy was gone. I stood and wondered why he had abandoned me. Then across the footbridge came a *carabiniere* patrol walking uphill towards me. I had not learned yet the equivocal position of the corps in their strange armed neutrality between Fascists, partisans and Germans. So I walked hard, not looking round, until I caught up with the boy waiting shamefacedly far up the hill.

The Russians came back the next day. Andrey was limping; his sock was holed and the boot had rubbed his foot raw. It was infected, red and angry with poison. In his pocket he had a black Beretta automatic. He had held up a staff car on the road, shot the officer and taken his gun. He was in high spirits though he could not get his boot on again. Sitting by the fire he told the story of Stalingrad and the two-pronged attack north and south of the town — two arms meeting round von Paulus and the German Sixth

Pebbles from My Skull

Army. I translated his story. Then the young boys danced with the peasant girls to the music of an accordion. It was warm; we had eaten well. In the midst of it all there was a visitor — the school-mistress from a little hamlet down by the main road. The peasants whispered together and with Lanciotto. She drank a glass of wine and talked with us — a woman in her forties with her black hair drawn back in a tight bun. I don't like her, said Andrey, Fascist. Lanciotto took her apart and signed to me to join him. We would not like to think you are a spy, he explained, if you are, you will be dealt with. She said: No, it was just that she knew the girls and wanted to drop in on them. She left before dark. We sat by the fire and sang Italian revolutionary songs: *Bandiera rossa* and *La Strada del Bosco*. Someone went out and came back with large flakes of snow melting in his hair. Bad, said Andrey, we won't be able to move. He drank hard and sang — *Katyusha*, *Stenka Razin* and *The White Whirlwind*. At midnight we walked over to the barn. The ground was white, with a thin layer of snow. The roof of the barn was coated with frost and shone like armour in the moonlight. It was 3 January 1944. Orion was at its midnight zenith, spread-eagled over the bare mountain. Andrey looked up and sniffed the air. I will never get home, he said.

Towards morning the sergeant-major woke me. He had risen to relieve himself and now brought me bolt upright with a whispered word: Fascists. We crawled about in the straw and shook the sleepers awake, muffling their protests with a hand over their mouths. There was a light at the bottom door and someone was saying to come out. Lanciotto signalled to me to go with him. We crawled along the top of the straw to the upper door and the machine-gun. The Sardinian was lying beside it with the butt into his shoulder and his finger on the trigger. Lanciotto crawled out before me on to the threshing-floor; we knelt under the cover of its low wall. We could hear the tramp of feet. Suddenly a group of militia, marching in threes, came out of the hollows of the hills Lanciotto gave me a sign to cover him and pulled the tag of a hand-grenade with his teeth.

The Savage Wood

They were quite close, their rifles still slung, when he threw it. When the explosion came, the machine-gun began to fire from inside the barn. A couple of short bursts. We saw the tracer pass a foot away. Then the gun jammed. The militia had broken ranks in a confusion of shouts and yells. Lanciotto stood up and harried them with grenades: Then we tried to get back into the barn. We could hear the Sardinian blaspheme. Another burst of fire forced us out on to the threshing-floor again. The gun jammed once more. We heard him tear off the magazine, swearing terribly. We threw ourselves past him and fell face down in the straw.

Inside it smelt of cordite. There was no noise except the singing and buzzing in my own ears. The lower door was clear. In the quiet of the first cold light I was seized with a wave of terror, like a child in the night stumbling on the thought of death. I looked at my watch. It was six o'clock. In a couple of hours, I thought, I shall be dead, and sat with my carbine on my knees automatically stuffing my pockets with rounds. I had a terrible wish not to be there, to be spirited away, to float up to the ceiling. So in childhood dreams, haunted by packs of wolves, I had drifted to safety. I had been frightened before — a sudden start which set the nerves tingling and sent the adrenalin flooding through me. This was a kind of whirling nausea, a desperate urge to tunnel in the straw, through the wall, the roof, to deny the reality of the pale light outside and the figures moving on the slope.

In the doorway the Sardinian was lying on his side wrestling with the jammed gun. I crawled over to him and looked out beyond the threshing-floor to a long slope of grass broken with patches of snow and grey stones. Now and again a stone seemed to move. Far down the slope someone was walking about gesticulating — an officer in a greatcoat wearing a helmet. I aimed and fired. The carbine kicked hard at my jaw. I did not see the strike of the bullet. So it went on, as the day cleared and the sun came out. From time to time our machine-gunner would fire a burst and then stop. Back would come an answering burst. They had

Pebbles from My Skull

the door covered. The low wall of the threshing-floor caught most of their fire. Once I felt a sharp blow on my arm. I looked down and saw my rifle-butt covered with blood. Reluctantly I examined my jacket. No hole, no pain. The blood, I saw with relief, was from a scratch between finger and thumb. The gunner fired again. I watched the ejected cartridge cases spin harmlessly past.

At the lower door the Russians and Lanciotto were firing at some invisible target. On the slope at my end there was a slow gradual movement uphill towards the barn. The firing became continuous. I was dazed with noise. Lanciotto came up and gesticulated. We were to break out at our discretion. I told the Sardinian. He said nothing but struggled to clear another stoppage. I went down to the lower door. Lanciotto was gone. The Russians were there and a couple of boys. One by one we ran crouching into the open and round the end of the barn where we dropped into a ditch by the side of the wall. There was nothing for the moment. About fifty yards away a militiaman came round the end of an outhouse, rifle in hand. He did not see us. I covered him and wondered whether to fire. Then he turned back and disappeared. We decided to get uphill. Andrey shook his head and settled down with his back against the gable wall and his rifle ready. He could barely stand for pain.

Above the barn, the hillside was suddenly naked and open. I ran fast with someone at my side, making for the cover of an outcrop of rock. A boy was lying on the grass on his back with his face a mask of blood. I jumped over him and went on. There were other bodies, alive or dead, lying on the slope. Behind the rocks I tried to control my pounding breath and let my eyes clear. The militia were creeping up from stone to stone. I fired, cursing the crude V-shaped back sight. I saw the soil beside me flick up in a series of little spurts. There was a pause. Then the spurts came again. A machine-gunner was ranging on me. The militia officer was standing in the open. I aimed and fired, aimed and fired. The chamber was hot in my hand. I wrenched at the bolt. Waited, wrenched at it again. It was jammed. Someone was

The Savage Wood

crawling along close to me. It was Mirko. He was shouting. Then I realized that the only movement was from down the hill. The bodies near us did not budge. No living body could lie so close to the earth. Mirko got up and began to run hard. I threw down my gun and began the long slow chase to the crest three hundred yards away.

On a barbed-wire fence just before the top I tore a deep scratch on my left wrist.

7

I do not know whether they fired on us all the way up the bare, withered mountain grass. I could hear nothing but the pounding of blood in my ears. My eyes seemed to bulge and to become suffused. My chest hurt intolerably. We did not slow our pace until we were on the other slope, looking down into the valley. There we rested for a moment. I saw to my astonishment that Mirko was wearing gym shoes. It was a cold bright day. Beyond Migliana, above the chestnuts and the beeches, the high Apennines were white and smooth. Below us there was a mill set on a long strip of land in the midst of the stream; a wooded crest ran down to the river. We set ourselves down among the trees, watched and waited. About midday a small boy scrambled down through the undergrowth and looked at us. Then he disappeared. An hour later he was back with a hunk of bread and some cheese. Were we in the fight? he asked. Yes. Stay here, he said, I'll tell my brother. In the late afternoon his brother climbed up from the mill. A smiling mill-hand of eighteen, quick, practical and cool. We must get you out of here, he said. Lanciotto is dead, so are the others. They are looking for 'the English captain'. But you killed some of them too.

A cold shadow began to fill the valley. We lay in the grass and shivered, discussing what to do. Mirko wanted to get down into the plain, to Sesto and the Party which was his love. I wanted to be alone, to depend on no one for my safety, to be my own sentry and watchdog. My instinct was to make for the hills, to hide and wait for the search to be called off. In truth I was bolting like a frightened animal, eager for warmth and shelter. As a compromise we agreed

The Savage Wood

to make for Migliana; there we would decide further. That night the boy from the mill guided us across the river and set us on our way. Before dawn we were asleep in the deserted farmhouse above the village.

There, next day, Diego found us. He had clambered up to visit a cow and her calf in the shed behind the house. A thickset, shambling man with a Punchinello nose and ruddy cheeks, he was famous for his *furbizia* — his peasant cunning. His motives — except when he had taken a person to his heart — were squarely based on self-interest. He could at will adopt a kind of idiocy that made him brother to the Good Soldier Schweik. Called up to serve in the cavalry, he had spent a few weeks dragging his hen-toed feet over the barrack-square, carrying pails of bran or watering the horses. But it was his boast that no one ever got him into the saddle. In time he was sent home, unfit for service. On his own hillside he was as nimble as a goat and stronger than most men. For wife he had chosen an elderly spinster with red, gummed eyes and a rich patrimony; the price he paid — apart from having her whine all day — was that he had to support her father, who sat by the fire, white-bearded and distinguished. *Molto signorile*, said his daughter. Diego calculated that the burden would not have to be long endured. As a man he was alternately stout friend and poltroon. Townsmen he hated, workers and politicians. Mirko and he detested each other at sight. A kulak, said Mirko. One of these madmen, said Diego.

A couple of days later Mirko left. His contempt for me was unspoken but unmistakable.

From the village Diego brought scraps of information. Lanciotto's body had been taken down into the valley and put in a hospital. Next day his two brothers and his wife arrived, fully armed, and removed it. The others were dead. The Russians had been bayoneted to death; the bodies dragged down into the valley behind an army truck. Of Ted there was no word. Franco had disappeared. One day Diego brought a cutting from the local paper. The obituary notice of a Fascist officer killed by 'bandits'. The word caught me

Pebbles from My Skull

between anger and contempt. I thought it over as I sat by my window and saw that, to the forces of authority the tactics of the resistance must always seem both cowardly and cruel. I knew now that the arms of the partisan must be inadequate, that he must compensate for his inadequacy by exploiting surprise, cunning and trickery. That the methods must range from the ambush to straightforward assassination. To come into the open and fight things out cleanly would be to invite destruction. I knew that he is constantly exposed to treachery and betrayal and must be pitiless to informers or even suspected informers.

This was as true of Italy as it is of today's anti-colonial wars.

That night Diego put a proposition to me. His brother, Ubaldo, lived in a tall house in the middle of the village. In a room on the top floor I would be able to live safe and unseen. But I must cut off all contacts with the outside world. I accepted thankfully, cravenly.

I came to know the house well. To reach it you climbed out of the village street on to a terrace; tall and narrow, the house backed on to a hillside. A steep path to the hills ran up past the gable-end. Its third, topmost storey looked clean over the valley. From the street there came the voices of women calling to their children and the clop of mules. I sat there all day long for four weeks. To distract me I had the view — the long sweep of the hills round the deep narrow valley, the chestnut forest with a few brown leaves twirling here and there, and above them the bare beeches on the skyline. Over the shoulder of the hill, where the road climbed a crest before falling down to Prato, I could just see the roofs of a hamlet. Closing the valley, across the river, was the long slope of the Calvana. I could trace the way we had come running down through the outcrops of rock, and guess where the barn must lie, behind the ridge — ruined now and blackened with fire; the farmhouse empty, looted, the menfolk jailed in Florence. The cloud patterns moved over the Calvana to Monte Morello. When there's a hat on Morello, I learned, peasant, take your umbrella.

The Savage Wood

*Quando Morello
mette il cappello,
contadino, prendi l'ombrello.*

I was not alone, sitting back from the window, unobserved in the winter sunshine. Caterina was often there. A girl of my own age, she had on her the marks of enduring spinsterhood. In her heart she hankered after a vocation. At half-past three each night she woke to the sound of her alarm and told her beads. One of the cult of the perpetual rosary, she had been allotted this cold hour for her devotions — a link in the chain of men and women praising the Virgin at each minute of the day and night around the world. Each morning she went fasting to Communion. That she could sit alone with me in the same room, she explained, was entirely due to the exceptional circumstances. Beneath her piety there lay the capriciousness of an old man's youngest, late-born daughter, convent-educated, spoilt by her brothers, denied nothing.

Sitting over some piece of embroidery she would interrogate me on *mores*.

Would you allow your fiancée to dance with another man?

Would you let your wife wear a low-necked evening-dress?

Would you let your wife go out by herself?

Before you were married, did you sit in the same room as your fiancée — alone?

Did you kiss her?

Then she rummaged in her long plain wooden dower-chest and produced a piece of underwear, embroidered by her own hand.

Aren't they nice?

Aren't they refined?

'Refined' was her favourite word — *fine, molto fine*. It applied to persons, to clothes, to taste, to the women of Florence, to knickers and to young priests.

Nationalism had bitten deeply into her.

Pebbles from My Skull

Had I seen any country as beautiful as Italy — the garden of Europe?

Was not Verdi the greatest composer who had ever lived?

Had I heard of Puccini? Madam Butterfly?

How could I, an Englishman, think that Beethoven was a great musician?

Wasn't Dante the greatest poet in the world?

Shakespeare? You only say that because you are English.

She catechized me on my faith.

In England you are not Christians.

I denied it.

Your priests marry; they cannot be Christian.

I remonstrated.

Then what do they believe?

I tried to explain Presbyterianism.

You mean you choose your own priest?

Something like that, I said.

Are you a believer?

I was brought up as one.

Then what are you now?

An agnostic.

Then you will go to hell.

The thought evidently pained her. I shall pray for you every morning, she said. What a pity — you have some of the temporal virtues but none of the cardinal ones; faith, hope and charity.

Sometimes her mother listened. Leave him alone, Caterina, she would say, maybe he's good in his own way. That's all that matters.

Her mother was tall and gaunt, with deep eyes and a black vein, permanently distended, like a blister at the corner of her mouth. Her hands were hooked into claws from years of washing in the icy water of the fountain. She hid them under her apron where she clasped against a belly, misshapen from many pregnancies, a little earthenware basket of glowing charcoal. She was, I suppose, in her fifties. She might by her looks have been sixty or seventy. Of her husband, dead these twenty years, she still spoke in

The Savage Wood

awe — *un vero signore*, owning half the village, leaving to his sons and daughters a rich patrimony. You should have seen him, she said, driving to the market with his horse and trap and everyone saluting him. *Molto bell'uomo, sa.* Now in her widowhood, a tertiary of the Franciscan order, she shared in a more restrained way in her daughter's piety. Asking her once why she sheltered me, I had this for answer: Because in the Gospel it says that we must feed the hungry and succour those in need. I would do the same for a German in your case — or a Fascist. You were all born of woman. She was a person of great warmth and love, unafraid. But at times she brooded over me, bringing memories of my childhood and a desperate desire to escape.

She, Caterina and I, shared the top floor. Downstairs past the privy, a hole with a round marble lid, lived her eldest son, Ubaldo, a thin, choleric man, bitter with life, with the war, with Fascism, with the Allies. I had never known a man so intemperate, so utterly of one humour. When he spoke of the workers in the valley he spat and choked with rage. Crossed in some petty detail by his wife, he swore horribly, coupling the name of the Virgin with dog and pig and whore, while his womenfolk stopped their ears with their aprons. He took it amiss that now, at the hardest moment of the war, his wife should be near her term. He hated Franco as an upstart ex-peasant and held him responsible in some obscure way for the decline of his own fortunes. In the black market he drove a hard, merciless bargain. Before the war they did nothing for us, these townspeople, he would say, I make them pay for it now. He thought me a fool to have got mixed up with the partisans — a lot of good-for-nothings who were afraid of a hard day's work. Let them come here with a hoe in their hands and I'll show them what work is. We Italians need a dictator. There's no discipline any more, no order. Now when my father was alive, we were a nation.

At the week-ends his sisters came up from the valley to collect flour, salami, eggs or a piece of illegally slaughtered veal. Elena was the eldest — the worn, plain wife of a

Pebbles from My Skull

white-collared clerk in some Prato factory; she hated the Anglo-Americans and rejoiced over the long bridgehead battle at Anzio. I would see; the Germans would win. They had the men and the guns and the power. Her husband she never brought with her; she was conscious of having married below her station. Ester was the middle one. Esterre, they called her; Tuscans cannot bear a word to end in a consonant. In her late thirties, she was plump and comfortable, with sudden moods that betrayed her sexual discontent. Childless and barren, she played the spoilt child and planned to spend Easter at Viareggio. If these Anglo-Americans would only hurry. At Viareggio she would sit under a huge umbrella in a black bathing costume with a scooped neckline. Did I want to see? She drew a photograph from her handbag. Caterina exclaimed at such licence. But Ester merely said: They all do it. Her interest in dress was obsessive; her life, planned round appointments with her dressmaker. *La sarta.* She knew little shops in Florence where they made beautiful lace and lovely lingerie. Between shopping she took tea at Doney's. Her husband, a soft, weak, good man, manager of a small factory, denied her nothing, paying daily for his lack of virility. A young man on holiday in the mountains, he had seen her at Mass and desired her. First he sent a formal declaration. Her mother studied it and approved. A formal reply acknowledged the declaration and asked for the name of the young man's confessor. The village priest took up the ghostly reference. The result was satisfactory. The pair were allowed to meet in public, to become engaged. The dowry was arranged. They were photographed arm in arm picking grapes, biting coyly at the same bunch. They were first alone on their wedding night.

On Sundays the house was full. We ate in the room where usually I sat alone. In the midst of the floor was a great earthenware pot full of glowing charcoal. We sat with our feet to it, and waited for the meal to begin. First, pasta made by the women of the house. (I had watched them at it, hollowing out a crater in a pyramid of sifted flour, breaking

The Savage Wood

eggs into it, mixing the dough, rolling it, folding it, rolling it again and folding again, until it dangled over the sides of the table, drying it by the window, cutting it into strips that curled like elastic in an old-fashioned milliner's.) Then boiled meat. Then roast with fried potatoes and perhaps a vegetable. Then wizened grapes, pears and cheese. Cheese and pears we ate together. I said how good they tasted. Each time came the stock answer: Don't tell the peasant. He'll eat them up. The inevitable rhyme:

> *Al contadino non si deve far sapere*
> *Quanto è buono il cacio colle pere.*

When Diego recited it the 'c's' were deeply aspirated. So I learned the Tuscan dialect with its wide open vowels and its sudden swooping drop through almost a whole octave to stress a syllable. *La calata*, they called it, the dip.

On weekdays I was often alone. To read I had:

Horace's *Odes*, Book IV — Ester's husband had thumbed them in school;

The One You Must Not Love — an erotic Italian novel; subject incest; provenance unknown;

The Prisoner — a novel by Lajos Zilahy, translated from the Hungarian; the adventures of a prisoner-of-war in Russia, 1914–18; belonged to Ester; good conventional fiction.

A school reader full of quotations from the Duce and poems in praise of bread: the mystique of a non-protein diet.

La Divina Commedia with Daumier's illustrations, read and understood now for the first time.

A school edition of the same with notes.

I sat at the cold window and looked across the river to Monte Morello. The river, I now knew, was the Bisenzio. Alberto degli Alberti held his lands in the valley. His two sons, Alessandro and Napoleone, fought to the death over the inheritance. In *Caina* Dante placed them — the icy circle

Pebbles from My Skull

in the very pit of hell. The ice clasps them together and freezes their tears before they can even roll down from their eyes. Their hair grows together into a frozen knot.

The charcoal brazier beside me glowed and winked. The monoxide fumes clouded my head. I had a passionate desire to walk out into the open air. Instead, to put some circulation into my feet, I padded to and fro in carpet slippers on the red tiled floor and cast my spiritual accounts. There is a moment in life when we recognize the patterns of our own behaviour. I had escaped unscathed from the desert battle; I had got away with a scratch on the wrist from the barn on the Calvana. Was this luck? Was 'luck' another way of saying that I contrived to survive where others died?

There were other questions to answer. Why had I not insisted that they post sentries? After the first failure I had not tried again because the command and the responsibility were not mine. Yet Lanciotto respected my professional advice. Had I argued he might have listened to me.

Should I have shot the militiaman as he came round the end of the outhouse — so near that I could see each detail of his uniform? I could hardly have missed. But if I had, would he not have caught us huddled together in a tight bunch under the wall of the barn? The duty of a soldier, I remembered, is to kill as many of the enemy as possible.

Should I have waited longer before rising from among the boulders on the hillside to begin the lung-tearing run up the hill? I did not think so. But I should never have thrown away the rifle, jammed or not. There was nothing wrong with it that an armourer could not mend in a couple of minutes. The patrols that came after us must have found it. Now the enemy had another gun. Small gain to them. To the partisans a disproportionate loss.

The snow came, blocking the hill roads and muffling the feet of the mules. But before that Ubaldo's wife was delivered of a daughter, born in the middle of the night. The day before was spent boiling water and storing it in old wine flasks, the necks stopped with cotton wool. I slept through her cries, sunk in the leaden, oppressive sleep which had

The Savage Wood

become usual with me, in the big hard bed under the holy water stoup and the black framed photograph of the man who would have been the child's grandfather, bearded, forbidding, *molto bell'uomo*.

I looked out over the snow and nursed the scratch on my wrist, which festered and would not heal. I wrote verses and committed them to memory. I thought of home but could summon up only a very generalized nostalgia. After three years' absence I found I had no strong feelings. The next months were too problematic, the chances too remote; my mind baulked at such a leap in time. Meanwhile I was developing melancholia, sudden fits of black depression, such as I had not known since the worst days in prison camp — the kind of mood that had made a man throw down his cards and leave the game without a word, to wrestle with himself in some sheltered corner, a blanket drawn over his face. Caterina's mother was quick to feel these attacks. With her little pot of hot ash under her apron she would stand over me and lament. Then great waves of claustrophobia swallowed me and I felt that I must, this moment, get out, move, be in the open, act.

One night Diego came stumbling up the stairs to see me. He had met Franco in the village. Did Diego know where Carlino was? Diego had lied with peasant skill but Franco knew him too well. He happened to know, he said, that I was in the top room of Ubaldo's house. He wanted to see me. It was up to me, said Diego. I said yes. An hour later Franco was there, laughing as usual. Diego is *furbo*, he said, but I am more *furbo* still.

First he brought news. Ted was in Florence waiting for a courier to take him over into Switzerland. The Germans were rounding up men to work on a great line of fortifications from coast to coast; it ran through the mountains just beyond Migliana. There was a partisan formation on the hilltop above the beeches; I could see the place from the window. They were in a strong position with good arms, well-built huts and a wall of turf fortifications round the camp. He himself was going to cross the lines with a

Pebbles from My Skull

message from the Committee of National Liberation. I had three choices. I could join Ted, join the partisans, cross the line with him.

I said I would cross the line, suppressing in my mind a sceptical doubt that he should have been chosen for so important a mission. We shook hands. He would come back in a few days with documents. He would dress me decently, then we would go by train as far as possible. The rest of the way would be on foot — through the Abruzzi.

For three or four days I waited. On one of them the sky was filled with a great drumming noise. High up, a formation of four-engined planes came flying over from the south. They flew very slowly. Watching them you had a sense of gravity, of full-bellied bomb bays. Something quite tiny — like a barrel — came tumbling out of the skies; then another and another. They fell just beyond the crest. I could see the roof-tops of a little hamlet vanish in a series of explosions. Everyone was very nice about it. The Americans, they said to comfort me as I sat looking over to the ruins, they don't bother to look.

At the end of the week the weather changed. The snow melted and the sun struck more warmly. Waking one morning, I heard voices in the house and footsteps running to and fro. The child, I thought. It had a fever and the cord was suppurating. Then I looked out of the window. On the other side of the valley, where the road came to a V, crossed a stream and turned towards Migliana, there was a column of militia with trucks and motor-cycles. They were debussing and shaking out into a line along the road, facing up towards the beeches. Whatever else happened they would search the village. I dressed quickly, found my school Dante, took my cloak and slipped out of the side door. Halfway up the path I met a couple of evacuees. They stood aside in astonishment as I scrambled past. I was above the houses and could look across the valley. There was firing. Mortar bombs were bursting on the slopes. I climbed and climbed. The air was fresh. There was sun. Flowers were showing between the grass. It was spring. I turned east and south and walked.

That evening, when the firing was over, the partisans temporarily scattered, and Franco taken, Diego searched the hills for me, weeping and calling my name. For days he looked for me in deserted huts, in caves and barns. Then he went back to his work. The Germans came, sweeping the hills to make a bandit-free zone round the Gothic Line above Migliana. Diego hid in the cesspit in the courtyard of his house, emerging hours later, covered with filth, stinking to heaven. Today he lives cannily with his blear-eyed wife. Ubaldo is less lucky, for he must wheeze his discontents through a hole in his throat until exhaustion forces him into angry silence. With a bitter smile he lifts a patch of gauze to show how, when cancer took him by the throat, they removed his larynx and left this makeshift mouth. He has seen the whole fabric of his society crumble away. Where his father was a man of substance, he is a labourer tied to his few remaining fields, struggling with tears and curses to keep his son at college with the Fathers, so that one day the boy may escape from the tyranny of the land. The price he will have to pay is this: the name of Santi will be forgotten in the valley. As for Caterina, five years ago she took the veil and in an Orvieto convent continues her vigils.

Franco the Gestapo took but did not break. Three years after the war I looked for him in vain in the cloth mills among the discarded uniforms from four armies, bales marked UNRRA, heaps of soiled rags. In the carding-rooms the unguarded machines tore and worried at them, shredding them into fibre for re-weaving as coarse-textured cloth. My guide was the manager — Elena's husband, Diego's brother-in-law. As we passed through the workrooms old friends from the village looked up from their machines and greeted me. The manager stood back disapprovingly. They were Reds, he explained. It might have been necessary to know them in wartime. In peace it was tactless. Whether Franco was a Red I never discovered. He claimed to have been a member of the Action Party, the group which promised so much in the Resistance and in the peace disintegrated so disastrously. What he did do, I

Pebbles from My Skull

learned, was to organize a cooperative store in the village, so winning the hatred of the village shopkeepers and their entire families — nieces, nephews uncles and aunts. In the cooperative he installed the village's first and only telephone. All conversations were public and monitored by the woman who served the shop. Now he lives in Prato, representative for a brand of rural gas.

The partisan fort is still there on the hilltop among the beeches — a low rampart of turfs. They held it intermittently until the summer of 1944 and the German retreat to the Gothic Line. Then they came down to surround a German outpost, forgot to cut the field telephone to the main force in the valley and were themselves surrounded, killed or captured. They were hanged in a village called Figline, above Prato, on the road to Magliana: Italians, Russians, Yugoslavs. The villagers watched as the ammunition boxes were kicked out from under the dazed battle-shocked men. The corpses swung from a beam under an archway, toes scraping the stone of the passage-way. At last someone in piety cut them down. Years later I saw the frayed strangling cords.

8

By midday I had crossed the road, the river, and the railway and was high up the slope of the Calvana. A charcoal-burner shared with me his bread and sheep's-milk cheese. We looked across to Migliana. There were little bursts of smoke high up among the beeches. The charcoal-burner saw me watching but said nothing; his complicity was absolute. When I left he wished me luck and looking across to the hills opposite cursed the regime and its tools.

On the crest of the Calvana I halted, facing Monte Morello, and plotted my route. It would take me in a wide arc round the back of the mountain and away from Florence. There would be the Sieve to cross. Beyond was the high plateau of the Pratomagno stretching away to the headwaters of the Arno and the central spine of Italy. From the heights I should be able, I reckoned, to see the Adriatic and the Tyrrhenian and, far south, the massif of the Abruzzi.

In the morning I had felt release, found an omen in the sudden smell of spring and the flowers pushing up through the grass on the hillsides. By evening the sensation had waned. For the first time I was travelling without Ted's laconic encouragement. I began to panic, wondering whether I should find anywhere that night to give me food and rest. At dusk I came to a farm on the far side of Morello. I knocked. I had a strange shame of begging, mixed with fear that I might be turned away. They took me in. They asked no questions. I ate at their table. After supper we talked. I discovered they had known the Russians. I told them the story of the fight in the barn. Before they went to bed the husband turned his chair round, knelt on it with one

Pebbles from My Skull

knee. The women and children were in a semi-circle by the dying fire. Together they said the rosary, mumbling and rushing the words in a strange chant. I felt the words strike home: *Ora pro nobis, nunc et in hora mortis nostrae, amen.* In the morning I thanked the woman of the house — her husband was out already cutting wood or fodder for the oxen. She watched me pick my path, standing long at the door before she turned back to her work. She and her like saved me from utter despair. Even so, for days and weeks I suffered a nightmare of loneliness in which I began to lose my resolution and my very sense of direction. I wandered aimlessly, caught in the folds of the hills. I trudged below a monastery on a mountain top — perhaps the Certosa; I was too disorientated to know. I found myself walking one morning past a country pleasure house of the Renaissance — some villa of the Medicis which I could not identify. Beyond it was a main road. I tested my nerve sitting on a gate and watching a German convoy pass. Then I crossed and like a wild animal chose the loneliest paths and roughest country. I found myself caught in a wilderness of thorns and brushwood. The path forked into a maze of dead ends. I sat on the swampy ground and wept with anger, despair and fear — not so much at the thought of dying as over the possibility that somehow I would disappear, vanish, be struck from the book of life.

One morning I found myself looking down on a river in a narrow valley. It was the Sieve. Now I had to decide. Whichever way I turned I knew I must cross a river; the Arno to the south, or the Sieve before me at my feet. I sat till noon on the hillside and pondered, savouring the spring sun, with my black cloak drawn round me. A girl came down through the trees driving a flock of sheep, greeted me and passed on. On the other side were the hills leading up to Vallombrosa and the Pratomagno. The river was not wide but quick-flowing. There was no sign of a bridge. I asked myself what I was doing walking on from day to day towards a front that seemed to be fixed immovably below Rome. Perhaps that was the Allied strategy — to draw the

The Savage Wood

German army down into the peninsula and grind it away in a war of attrition. I thought of the safe, easy life in a prison camp, with three meals a day, Red Cross parcels, mail, company, the schoolboy rags. St Anthony on a hillside, I was tempted by all devils except sex.

In the afternoon I got up and began to walk down the steep descent to the river. The path was well-trodden and must lead to a crossing-point — a ferry perhaps. Just before the river I met a peasant woman. We passed the time of day. I walked on. She called to me: Oh, young man, she said, if you are one of those I would not cross. There's a patrol waiting on the other side. I thanked her and turned along a path through the field by the river.

My quandary was this: if I walked downstream I would find myself in the town of Pontassieve, at the confluence of Sieve and Arno. If I crossed now I would be in full view of the road which ran along the farther bank. Something encouraged me — the smell of the water on the stones, and the familiar rush of the water, turning and swirling in deep trout pools. I walked on till the river was screened from the road by trees and bushes, took off my boots, socks, pants, trousers, bundled them in my shepherd's cloak, pulled my shirt up under my armpits and began to wade across. The water was chill with snow, but not too deep. The shock was bracing. The cold ache in my toes I remembered from the river of my childhood. I splashed out, bare-bottomed, and thought how ridiculous I must look to an observer on the hill behind me. On the bank I rubbed myself dry, dressed, and made off over the road.

Two days later I was floundering in muddy fields on a spur of hill running down from Vallombrosa. My depression was gone but I lacked the determination I used to have when, with Ted, I struck out each morning towards some distant landmark. So by evening I had made little progress. I had come right down to the side of the Arno, crossing a busy main road and a deserted railway. The fields by the river were empty. The path wound along a grassy bank. The water was full and fast, brown with mud. There was a

Pebbles from My Skull

hum of trucks from the road above me. The valley narrowed. The road went on, through a village, and up the valley towards Arezzo. The railway crossed the river by a girdered bridge. Between the steel lattice-work I could see the helmet of the sentry pass to and fro. I would wait for dusk, slip under the bridge and past the village. If the worst came to the worst there was a kind of broken weir where I might scramble across. As darkness began to fall, when the sentry turned towards the far end of the bridge I walked under the track. His feet rang on the metal overhead. There was a boat by the bank a hundred yards further on. A man in it was reaching for his oars. As I drew near he lingered, gave a short hissing signal, and a slight motion of the hand. I walked over and stepped into the stern of the boat. Without a word he pushed off and rowed to the other side. That's my house up the hill, he said. There I slept the night.

From the ferry, my track went zigzagging through the little hills beyond the Arno. Each day the weather seemed to improve; the men moved out into the fields to prune the vines. I began to understand how, in the Middle Ages, they had looked across the shortest day to the turning-point of the year, when life would be tolerable once more with a promise of food and fruit and crop's increase. But I took no part in the work of the fields. Like the Franciscans I met, with their mendicant's sack and bare sandalled feet, I was outside the society through which I passed. I had my face to the south and meant to go on, try to pass the line. I had become silent and farouche. I would move from one barn to another in the night and disappear next morning without food or a greeting. Sometimes I would lie up all day in a patch of heath and sleep or read Dante and wait for the time to pass. I was a connoisseur of byres and sleeping-places. Warmest were the deep piles of beech or chestnut leaves in which I sank up to my neck and felt the warmth over my body. Chaff was the worst — too short for comfort, it had no heat in it and filled my clothes with little needles of straw. Best of all was a heap of sacking and a covering of hay in the corner of a byre with the breath of

The Savage Wood

the oxen to take the chill from the air.

Lying in such a corner, in a little byre with a couple of young oxen, I woke to feel something — rat or mouse — moving at my feet. I wriggled my toes and turned over to sleep. It came again — something warm and searching, moving over the soles of my feet. I sat up and struck a match. As the flame sprang out a young ox left licking at my socks with its rasping tongue, leapt off all four feet and charged to and fro. The match burnt down to my fingers. In the darkness I felt for my boots and my cloak and slid along the wall to the door. I could hear the click of horns as the ox stood listening, swinging its head and breathing heavily. The door was bolted on the outside; the peasant had run the wooden cross-bar quietly home as he left me for the night. I pulled on my boots and kicked at a plank. It gave a little, I could hear the beast scraping the floor with its hooves. I kicked again and the plank came away with a squeal of rusty nails. Another kick and there was a narrow gap. I squeezed through, gathered my cloak round me in the cold night and walked on.

Thus aimlessly I drifted south through a moraine landscape and into Chianti. The ruined towers guarding the valleys I came through were frontier posts from the days when Florence marched with Siena. A little stream I crossed was the Arbia. I knew it from my Dante. One day it had run red with blood — *colorata in rosso* — when Farinata degli Uberti, the great Florentine traitor, with Sienese militia and German mercenaries, cut down his fellow-townsmen at the battle of Montaperti. From his burning tomb the great heresiarch rose and challenged Dante with the question: 'Who were *your* forebears?'

Looking from the edge of a wood I saw Siena clumped on its hills; the bell tower stretched up against a pale sky. In the far distance, closing the landscape, a mountain floated over a pale haze. The Monte Amiata.

For the first time the peasants were inhospitable. I wandered through the woods and felt the sharp eyes of the shepherd girls upon me. A woman gave me a piece of bread

Pebbles from My Skull

but when I asked to sleep in the straw said her man was out in the fields. At last an old man took me in, gave me supper and led me down into the byre. In the middle of the night I awoke with a light shining in my face. Gradually I made out someone standing over me in a long black cloak.

Who are you? he asked in Italian.
Someone passing through.
What are you doing?
Sleeping.
Who are you?
Suppose you tell me.
The man groped for a word.
You're not Italian, I said.
What are *you* then?
English. And you?
South African.
Then what the hell are you playing at?
Man, you can't be sure.
Well, now bugger off and let me sleep.
See you in the morning, man.

The morning brought him down to waken me — broad, powerful, with the build of a prize-fighter. He had a constantly worried air — a look of anxiety in his eyes, as if he found his situation too much for his limited intelligence. His poor mind was flawed through and through by racial hatred. As we climbed up the steps of the house to breakfast he spoke of the old man: Not a bad Kaffir, he said. The old man was at table with his daughter, a good-natured, slightly dishevelled girl in her twenties. Her husband was a prisoner of war. In India. Who knows whether they will get enough to eat there? Is it near England? No? South Africa? Anyway let's hope that someone will do to him what we try to do for Piero here. He's been here for months — a good workman. Speaks like one of us.

Born in the bilingual culture of South Africa, Piero had learned to speak with the true Sienese accent. He was one of a group from a work camp. At the armistice they had moved in to live with the peasants whose fields they had

84

The Savage Wood

worked as prisoners. With many of the young men missing they were drawn into the peasant economy, were now part of the family. We would go and see some of the others later, he said. We went to his bedroom. He dressed with care, combing and recombing his hair. There was a book on the window-sill. I opened it automatically. A Dutch Reformed Bible. I turned the pages looking for a familiar text — 1 Corinthians 13. Can you read it? he asked. Yes, I replied, it's quite like German.

We walked down towards the Arbia to a farmhouse set in meadows by the stream. There was a haze of green on the trees by the water. The buds were bursting with a tip of green here and there, sexual, swelling. In the long, low kitchen we found a tall blond giant South African whom the Italians had dubbed Filippo. He had huge boxer's hands and a weak handsome face. When we came in he was sitting on a bench by the table with his arm round the waist of a young, dark girl with the liquid ox-eyes of Homer's goddess. She was plump and soft, yielding. Her mother turned from bending over a pot on the fire and greeted me. He's like a son, Filippo, she said, and after the war they'll get married. The bloom on the girl's face was that of her first pregnancy.

From Filippo we learned that 'the captain' wanted to see me. It was a long walk through woods and across rocky hillsides. The valley of the Arbia coiled and twisted at our feet, green and enclosed. A woodpecker cackled and swooped across a clearing. As we walked they questioned me.

It was the kind of conversation I had had a hundred times. What's your regiment? what battalion? what Corps? As I answered I became aware of my predicament, for they had heard of none of them. How could they? My battalion had gone from the East African campaign to Iraq and Cyprus. As for the Corps headquarters on which I had served, it had arrived in the desert after they were already prisoners. They spoke together in Afrikaans before trying another tack. What South African units did I know? The Transvaal Scottish, I said, and the Kaffrarian Rifles. What about the

Pebbles from My Skull

police battalions? I had never heard of them; in any case my job was to know about German units, not Commonwealth ones.

We walked on in silence.

Captain Barbi was waiting in the farm on a little plateau. The peasant's wife had poured him a glass of wine; there was bread and salami on the table. She stood to one side with her hands in her apron, a big fat woman with a soft face, worn, but with merry eyes. When I appeared she withdrew. The captain indicated that I might sit down. He was a man in his thirties, good-looking, carefully tended moustache. Slightly pompous.

Well, he began, who are you?

I told him my name and added that, in Italian, I was called Carlino.

All right, Carlino, prove it.

You'll have to take my word. I have no papers.

Naturally, he said. How did you get here?

I traced my route.

And where are you going?

I don't know exactly — over to Arezzo and the headwaters of the Arno.

You're a bit out of your way, aren't you?

I agreed.

How do you know Tuscany so well?

I can read a map.

Where did you learn Italian?

At the university.

Where?

In Scotland.

You have a slight accent — a funny 'r'. Almost German.

He got up and withdrew into the window with the South Africans. They whispered together. He came back and began to question me once more.

They say you should have an officer's identity card.

I destroyed it when I was captured.

They have never heard of your Corps.

I'm not surprised.

The Savage Wood

They don't know your regiment either.
I don't suppose they would.
You can read Dutch.
Yes, I speak German.
He paused and thought.
Is there anyone who can vouch for you?

Send a messenger to Campi, near Florence. Ask for the butcher. Lanciotto's the name. You'll find a widow in the shop. Her husband was killed on the Calvana on January the third. She knows me.

All right, he said. We'll see. Now we'll get a place for you to stay.

We went down the hill together to a farm at the end of a cart track. It looked down on the dusty road to Siena and a hump-backed bridge over the Arbia. Beyond it the valley opened out into water meadows. There ten days later the captain called.

It's all right, he said. She says you must be Carlino and sends her greetings. It's just as well. We would have had to shoot you.

The Sweet Season

si ch'a bene sperar m'era cagione
. . .
l'ora del tempo e la dolce stagione

So that the hour of the day
and the sweet season . . .
moved me to good hope.

Inferno, I, 41–3

9

For ten days I had been content to stay in one spot under surveillance and an unspoken threat. Yet it would have been easy enough to evade my custodians; slip away through the woods, over the hills and down into the Arno valley. What kept me was a kind of fatalism combined with a feeling that I had at last found a roof, shelter, human companionship. So I took a chance on the messenger, walked by the Arbia and waited. People came to inspect me. Major Terosi came down from his estate — small, ginger-haired, with a Yorkshire mother, an honest man, conscious of his duties as a land-owner. War was his profession but he had been unable to exercise it. His English blood had kept him off the active list. Now he had grouped round him Captain Barbi, and a young parachute lieutenant, monarchists both of them. His cousin came cycling up the cart track, a good-looking woman in her thirties; educated at some English girls' school, she spoke English with me and tested my accent. At night I slept in a bed and in the morning I shaved with warm water, boiled on the fire. From the window over the sink I watched the German convoys pass down towards Siena in a little cloud of white dust.

To see the farm properly you had to climb up to the spring. The land crabs scuttled through the wet grass and plumped into the water. *Granchi* they were called and from them the place had its name: Le Granchiaie. A long, two-storeyed building, screened with trees. Little airless windows under the eaves. The front door stood at the top of the flight of stone steps. They led into the long kitchen with its wooden table, the flour chest by the wall, the sink, and the deep fireplace. On one side of the fireplace a door led

Pebbles from My Skull

into '*la camera*', the bedroom where husband and wife slept with their nine-year-old daughter. It was the only room in the house to be furnished in any formal sense, with a cheap bedroom suite the wife had brought as her dowry. Upstairs were three bedrooms — one for the peasant's unmarried brothers; one for his mother and sister; one, unused, which became mine. It was my home for nearly six months; here I ate, slept, and grew into the family.

The peasant was Dino; too old for active service he had been posted to a coastal battery. He had not, he was glad to say, seen a shot fired in anger. At the first opportunity he had come straight home. He had a wry twisted smile and a gentle cynicism. In his laconic way he reminded me of the ploughmen of the Angus valleys. Nella was his wife, plain, laughing, unperturbed, full of wonder at the stories she heard the menfolk tell round the table after supper. Her one passion was her nine-year-old daughter Graziella; for her she was always finding a fresh ribbon, washing a frock or cooking some titbit. Her two brothers-in-law might have been from different stock, so disparate were they in looks and temperament. Enzo was small, dark and thin, with a quick intelligence. In the army he had become fascinated by engines. In the byre, under the kitchen, he had rigged up an apparatus to drive the mixer in which, morning and evening, they cut the feed for the oxen: a simple, effective chain-drive worked by pedals from an old bicycle. He had plans for a dynamo some day. Meantime he tinkered with an old crystal set and lay in bed at night searching for a signal. Carlo was burly with a round clown's face, immensely strong. He was a practical joker who would chase his sister Maria round the kitchen with a dead mouse or watch grinning as his half-blind mother searched for the wineglass he had hidden from her. He had been called up but had no intention of reporting to his regiment.

Maria was twenty-three, old to be unmarried, engaged to a little man with a face like a ferret who had a poor farm far up the valley. She had no love for him. What do you want me to do, Carlino? I have to get married sometime. I can't

The Sweet Season

live here till I'm an old maid. There's no one else who wants me. She was well-built, tough and lithe. When she smiled, her upper lip wrinkled to show her strong, white teeth. She was out all day in the woods herding the sheep, with her distaff under her arm and an apronful of wool to be spun. Or else she would come walking through the fields with a sickle in one hand and on her head a basket of herbs and grass for the rabbits in the hutch under the stairs. Or climb past the walnut-tree and cherry-tree to the spring to sink her copper jugs deep into the cold water and, as she waited for them to fill, smile up to where I sat among the branches. In the morning she would wake me as she woke her brothers. She was frank, open, laughing, with brief sadnesses that she shook off with a sudden toss of the head. We held each other in absolute trust and true affection.

The real head of the house was the grandmother — *la nonna*. Half blind with cataract, toothless, given to drinking surreptitious glasses of the house's thick, strong wine, she kept a close check on the business of the farm. By nature she was deeply pessimistic, prophesying woe by the fireside. In her immediate domain was the care of the chickens and the cheese-room. When the sheep came in from the woods it was she who milked them — a hazardous task for it must be done *a tergo*. The bowl filled indiscriminately with milk and droppings. The milk she curdled with a herb from the garden. The whey she strained off and set on one side to be boiled gently till it formed a soft, spongy, white mass of *ricotta* with an indeterminate taste like the ghost of sour milk. The cream cheese she squeezed into shape in narrow, earthenware moulds. These she inspected daily, smelling the cheese, forcing the last drops of moisture from it with her old, crooked, dirty hands, lamenting that nothing was so good as it used to be, that her broody hen had lain under a hedge somewhere, that a hawk had been at her chickens, that the rabbits were hungry, and the war had gone on too long. She found in me a listener detached enough not to mock her like her sons, or have sudden bouts of impatience like the women of the family. Sitting by the fire she would

Pebbles from My Skull

catechize me on my past, understanding little, confusing places, facts, dates, weaving out of it all a legend. This, she would say, rolling her purblind eye until the red showed beneath the eyeball, this is my fourth son.

Soon I knew the rhythm of their lives. Monday was the day for baking. The oven at the end of the house was raked out and crammed with bales of brushwood. They roared and sparked for an hour. When the door was opened there was a thick layer of red-hot wood ash on the floor of the oven; the walls glowed with constellations of fiery stars. The dough had lain under a quilt overnight while the yeast worked in the warmth. The women slapped and shaped the loaves, then ran them into the oven on a long wooden shovel. The bread was flattish, round, a little brown from the coarse-ground flour, and saltless. Next day the ashes were raked out. Sprinkled between the home-made linen sheets in the huge earthenware washing-tub, their alkali bleached the bedding white. Then the women spread the sheets on the slope beside the cherry-tree and let the spring sun finish the job. Between times they worked with the men in the fields, breaking off to cook a meal or to gather herbs in the fields — bitter sorrel, chicory, or dandelion leaves for salad. Their one fear was illness; their ignorance of medicine almost complete; the country doctors, negligent and greedy, demanding to be paid in full for black market petrol before they would visit. So while I was drawn into the net of illegality they went about their business as the menfolk did about theirs — ploughing, weeding between the vines, grafting, pruning. With deep courage and admirable stoicism they followed the cycle of the year, drawing strength from the necessity which lies behind growth and blossom, fruition and harvest. The front might be moving but there were the vines to spray. They looked beyond the battle which must pass over their fields and planned for the coming year. War they faced as they faced old age and death.

I envied them their deep-rooted attachment to the land and came back to them always as a fixed point where I could

The Sweet Season

find rest, shelter. I tried to avoid compromising them and went unarmed about the farm. But at table I sat facing the door with, on my right, the stairs to my bedroom and the sub-machine-gun under the quilt. Sitting after supper at night, drinking the wine and talking, we would hear footsteps outside and wait for them to come up the steps to the door. It was always a bad moment before the door opened to some harmless visitor — a pedlar with his pack, Maria's fiancé, a girl bearing some piece of intelligence, reporting a car on the road or a stranger on a woodland path.

It was thus the shepherd girls had reported me when first I crossed the Arbia. With the incredible swiftness of peasant intelligence, word had gone round the network of the Resistance to boycott me and to make me harmless. The nucleus was a group of ex-prisoners gone soft, most of them, with easy living over winter. South Africans chiefly with the deep inferiority complex of the men who had surrendered at Tobruk. They were narrow, tough, ignorant. They ate at the peasants' tables, slept with their daughters, and scoffed at them in Afrikaans. The best of them was 'Gino', a tall, red-haired boy from Durban. A little simple, he was utterly unselfish and brave enough to conquer his own fears. The peasants loved him. Soon I had located them all, walking for miles across country to search them out and brace them for the last months before the front passed over us. I had found, too, a couple of Tynesiders, canny and distrustful, until I sang as best I could *The Blaydon Races*. It was not much of a force. They had between them a few Italian sub-machine-guns, some ancient revolvers, relics of the previous wars. One had a walking-stick with a tiny pistol in the handle. They had not more than a couple of dozen rounds between them.

Now that I was of their number I began to learn their secret paths and meeting-places, the stony footways through the vineyards, the stepping-stones on the Arbia, the secret pools in the close valleys, the long walk up through the woods to the flour-mill. I met the miller — a

Pebbles from My Skull

thin, wasted man covered from top to toe in a white mould. He had a daughter, plump, freckled, whose husband was missing on the Russian front. As I sat at table, drinking her father's wine she would come and brush lightly against me. There was a girl of twelve or thirteen — unexplained, neglected, some bastard of the family. Wild, with dark draggled locks, she had a cat's beauty. She sat by the fire, Cinderella-like, but not meekly. At a word she would flare up, throw the stick with which she poked the ashes into the heart of the glow, and slip out of doors. I met the peasant who kept a bull at stud. A man of blood, squat, in his late fifties, he had in his eyes a red flame from drinking too much wine and too much *grappa* — the wild, colourless grape alcohol. He wore defiantly his old Alpini hat with its eagle feather. High up on the limestone slopes of the Carso he had learned to kill Germans in the First World War. His one wish was to kill a few more. The bull munched in its stall, nose-ringed, silky, with a beautiful scrotum. Beside the house was the wooden frame in which they penned the cows that came to be leapt. His two daughters watched from the balcony and giggled. They were brazen hussies who obeyed only their father. Their mother, large, dark and handsome, shook her head at them as she fed the silkworms in an inner room. Baskets of mulberry leaves they ate. In the stillness you fancied you could hear the soft munching of a thousand jaws. In the kitchen the swallows nested, flying out and in at the window. The girls waited for the brood to hatch. They would fry the slug-like fledglings in oil. I kept well out of their way when I met them in the woods or in the pool in the little gorge under their house, where they sat in the cool water, splashing and squealing. But with their brother I shared a bed more than once. He was a weak-minded youth, repulsive in his personal habits. In the hot close nights he threshed about in his sleep, the prey to some wild dream.

Far afield — almost in the plain — I walked past a lignite mine (we ought, I determined, to raid it for explosives) and on to a great house with a long avenue of cypresses. The

The Sweet Season

owners were liberals and themselves in hiding; but the *fattore* was there, free and generous with food and wine for all who needed it. A widower, he lived in a small house at the edge of the policies with his only daughter. She was engaged — in some obscure way — to an Austrian officer but he had been posted from Italy. He had left his *fidanzata* a zither. She taught me to play and to sing of the hunter in the woods and his meeting with the peasant girl:

> *Era graziosa e bella,*
> *graziosa e bella,*
> *il cacciatore se n'innamorò.*

Nearer home, under the castle of Brolio, I met the man who kept the great wine cellars and learned about Chianti, fleeting the time carelessly as they did in the golden world.

I learned the way to the major's estate, walking up past the brushwood fences in the long ride through the woods where his mother had used to jump side-saddle. There I would meet the major's brother-in-law out cantering with his wife. At the sight of me they touched their horses' flanks with their spurs and rode off in a shower of turf from the hooves. They disapproved of me, their brother and his doings. Certainly there was about him something quixotic. His head was full of plans for seizing a village outside Siena and holding it until the Allies dropped reinforcements. We discussed the plan over a map in his office where the peasants came and went and the *fattore* kept the accounts. Captain Barbi was there and Silvio, the parachutist lieutenant. I do not know whether they were as terrified by the plan as I was. We sipped *vin santo* and discussed the war, argued over Allied strategy and the alliance with Russia. We decided that the major must make contact with the Committee of National Liberation in Siena and through them with the Allies. We would ask for arms.

One day the major came down to find me. He had made contact with the Allies. He had to meet a landing-party from a submarine near Grosseto. His wife had property in the Maremma, the wild coastal plain. He could travel down

Pebbles from My Skull

without attracting attention. Could I get the names of all the prisoners in the neighbourhood? A week later, he set off with pony and trap. In his pocket was a list of names and the coordinates of our dropping zone.

On the other side of the valley, in a little hamlet far off the road, I found the other side of the Resistance. Ferruccio lived there with some peasant relative — cousin or second cousin. This was not his true name, but so he was known to the Communist Party in Siena and to the network. He was a worker from a little engineering workshop in Siena — a man in his fifties, older than his age, fair-haired, a schemer, as busy in the black market as in the Resistance. A man I did not trust. He had a completely closed mind. Through him I met the commissar, a young dark man who had come out from Siena specially to meet me. I was to organize the prisoners, collaborate with the major, and make sure that they didn't just talk. He had brought me a present — a small, neat Beretta automatic and two clips of ammunition. We depend on you, he said. You know what will happen to you if things go wrong.

We met in the village cobbler's. A *carabiniere* who had fought the Germans at Rome's Porta San Paolo in the first confused days after the armistice, he had gone back to his old trade. I had other contacts scattered about in the villages and farmsteads where the Chianti hills came down to the plain. A Socialist lawyer with his wife and son in a cool villa — he hated Ferruccio passionately and feared him as much as the Fascists. A Jewish architect and his family in a remote farmhouse, their lives in the hands of the peasants. A chemist from Florence in a pleasant house on a hill looking towards Siena. He had a good table and a good radio — not sealed up by the authorities but tuned to London. I listened to the announcers and thought of them turning back through the night to home. In a peasant house a strange couple — a good-looking young woman (a seaside tart, Captain Barbi called her), and a silent young man. Police from Siena had called on them and left them undisturbed. Either they had good papers or they were agents. The

The Sweet Season

peasant, readily assuming the role of voyeur, reported that they spent most of the day in bed or reading. We judged these activities harmless.

One evening the captain sent a message to ask whether I could dine at a big house beyond the Arbia. We walked there together. There were stone lions at the gates; a long avenue carpeted thickly with pines with brown pine needles; beyond in the sheltered slopes the prickly pears were about to flower. They want to put their accounts right, said the captain cynically, before the Allies come. I have left word where we are. In case.

It was strange to sit in a drawing-room and drink vermouth. A courteous host, an old lady, scented, talking of London and garden parties before the war. Then the other guests arrived. The tart and her young man. At dinner I found myself beside him. The food was good. Homemade pasta. Veal. The Chianti was as it should be — strong and dry. My neighbour spoke little; his girl friend was charming the captain, who was unbending gradually. She had round protruding doll's eyes and round protruding breasts. Over coffee the young man was again at my side. I made some trivial remark.

You are an English officer, he said with a strong accent.

Yes, I said.

May I present myself? I am a German one.

Oh, yes, I said. Then why are you here?

He had been going on leave with his fiancée — he inclined himself in the direction of the tart. On the Brenner a superior officer had allowed himself to be disrespectful to the lady. Thereupon he had struck the officer and deserted.

Where were you before that?

On Rommel's staff. Liaison officer with the Italians.

What kind of guns had Rommel's personal defence force — the Kampstaffel Kiel?

Twenty-five pounders. I see you were in Intelligence.

We talked about the desert and its personalities — Major Bach, the Protestant parson who held out at Halfaya, Major-general Cruewell and how he crashed with the

99

Pebbles from My Skull

pilot's brains spattering his uniform. It was late and time to go.

Tell me, I said, what was the point of all this — to talk about the desert?

Do you think you could arrange — when the Allies arrive I mean — for me to be interned with my fiancée? We would hate to be separated.

I said I could give no guarantees.
We shook hands.

If, I said, as a result of tonight's talk, anything goes wrong, you know what will happen.

I shall not say a word. *Ehrenwort.*

As we walked down the avenue of pines, I told the captain my story. We laughed all the way to the crossroads where we parted.

10

Chianti is a geographical expression: three *comuni* go to form it — Radda, Gaiole, and Greve. Wild country in part with harsh grey outcroppings of rock on the hillsides, thick woods of chestnut and, on the hilltops, pines. In the valleys there are quick clear streams. The trout ripple the water in the shallows and in the deep pools sun themselves on rock ledges. Down towards Siena the valleys are green, narrow and close. In May and June they have a hothouse smell of warm, damp earth and luxuriant growth. The trees, hedgerows, and thickets are full of nightingales. They sit in the walnut-trees outside the farmhouse windows and drive away sleep. In the woods over the valleys the snakes move out into the sun and couple on the hot stone. The high broom in the woods crackles with bursting pods. Round the mill-ponds the frogs tumble into the water from among the high grass; the miller's geese hunt them in the reeds. Hawthorn and cherry blossom come and go. In the fields are wild poppies, sky-blue chicory, scarlet pimpernels, and wild irises — the lily badge of Florence. Beyond the fields, where the land falls to a plain the light lies in a thick golden haze. Far away the Monte Amiata rises in a pale blue mass. Here I first learned that Claude Lorrain did not exaggerate.

Chianti is a wine, sprung from the limestone of the hills, from grapes swollen by the close heat of the valleys. You may tell it by the black cock on the red label high up on the neck of the bottle. There is no other Chianti. The rest, I learned, is red Tuscan wine, cut — as like as not — with grape alcohol from the South, manufactured in factories for the tourist trade, for the foreign market, sold on the strength of some plaited straw and a round-bottomed flask.

Pebbles from My Skull

In the peasant houses the flasks are lined up in the cellar, uncorked, sealed with a layer of green olive oil, which you flick out on to the kitchen floor with a turn of the wrist. It is a dry wine, full-bodied, of thirteen or fourteen degrees.

Chianti is the place where I passed some of the best months of my life, bathing in cool hidden pools, walking the warm dusty roads in the dark, watching the land crabs in the spring and the cherries falling like gouts of blood on the stone where Maria set her pitcher. Blue jays in the woods and green woodpeckers; wagtails in the streams; hawks dangling over the meadows. In the dark, owls and startled pheasants rising with a cackle from the brushwood. Fireflies in the green wheat. In my closed hand their cold point of light made a pink transparency of the skin. Graziella ran into the dusk to catch them, calling them to her with an old rhyme, promising them bread fit for kings and queens:

> *Lucciola, lucciola,*
> *vien' da me,*
> *io ti darò il pan' del re,*
> *il pan' del re e della regina,*
> *lucciola, lucciola, vien' vicina.*

One evening the shepherds from the Maremma passed on their way to the high Apennine to spend the summer on the short-grassed pastures. Through the winter and the lambing they had kept their flocks among the Etruscan tombs. They slept in the hay. In the morning they paid their lodging in milk and curds and moved slowly on, tall men in long black cloaks, taciturn and close. Their dogs were always at heel lolling their tongues — gaunt, shaggy, with a spiked collar on their lean necks.

I had reached a point of equilibrium which allowed me to take each day as it came and look no further than the next. I was fitter than ever before in my life, covering such distances in a day that the peasants heard me with polite incredulity. I knew what I was doing. Was no longer alone. Had responsibilities that time or bad luck were bound to cancel — one way or the other. I was, I thought, grappling

The Sweet Season

with reality — giving the lie at last to the terrible text I had learned from my father in tears and despair: 'Unstable as water, thou shalt not excel' (Genesis 49:4). Being caught in illusion, it did not occur to me to think that war can be a bloody holiday. At the back of it all, never admitted, the chance, sudden perhaps, perhaps almost painless, of escape from the problem of living. Some things disturbed me. When the miller's daughter with a face freckled like burned trout looked at me across the hearth, stooping at the fire so that her breasts swung gently in her open blouse, I felt the sudden movement of the blood. Now in my second year of celibacy I found the condition harder to bear than when cloistered behind wire. Some nights I slept in her house, in the room over the mill-wheel. Under my window the mill-race threw spray up the wall like a bow-wave. The building creaked and groaned like a ship at sea. I listened in the dark and was tempted to rise and find the room where she wearied for her husband, lost and missing in the wars. If I turned over and pulled the sheet over my face it was not from virtue but to avoid complication.

Now for the first time I lost my fear of the dark and grew to welcome it as a friend and protector. Walking through the woods and along the pathways in the broom I felt that I moved in absolute safety, in a cloak of darkness. I learned the soft flight of the owl — less a noise than a muffled movement of the air. I saw the water-meadows by the Arbia fill with white mist through which, guided by the rush of the water, I walked waist-deep to find the stepping-stones. Once, after curfew, tramping home through the rain of a warm spring night with a huge green peasant umbrella over my head, I saw headlights sweeping the curves of the road behind me, sidestepped over the verge, jumped a low dyke, and parachuted down ten feet into a field below. Overhead the lights came and went and the noise of the engine died away. I lay in the dark field, rubbed my bruises, and rolled about laughing. Once in the night I was seized with real panic. A German motor-cycle patrol had stopped at a crossroads, forcing me to cut through the

Pebbles from My Skull

major's woods. There was a stream — almost dry with barely a trickle of water between the stones; overhead blackberry and sloe bushes arched into a tunnel. I had often come that way by day. Now in the dark moonless night I found myself trapped and held by long vicious sprays which whipped across my face and fastened in my clothes. Forward or back there was no way through. I could hear the motor-cycle engine phutting gently a few hundred yards away. I began to scramble desperately among the stones. The din seemed enormous. The dark was suffocating and armed with claws. At one point it seemed to thin a little and I tore my way forward. I came out on the dew-soaked grass and lay there, sore and frightened, till my heart began to beat more calmly. The motor-cycle had gone. I walked home across the field. Arcadia was crumbling.

With each day the movement on the roads increased. Single trucks, trains of lorries, of horse-drawn waggons. At night the drivers picketed their horses among the vines. In the morning they were gone, the vine-shoots nibbled bare. By day the Allied fighters patrolled the country ways. They glinted as they stooped over the low hills, level with the ruined watch-towers. The noise of their cannon was like pneumatic drills. They shot at any moving thing.

At a peasant with his oxen and cart. The driver flopped unscathed into a ditch. The dead beasts were steaks for the black market.

At a truck loaded with contraband sugar. The peasants were on it like ants, staggering off up the hillside paths with hundredweight bags on their shoulders. The children swept the road where a sack had fallen, split open by a cannon-shell, and ate in sweet handfuls.

At a little black Fiat. The driver and his passenger rose from the roadside, searched the bullet-riddled wreck, made a hurried fire by the roadside and burnt a handful of papers. They scattered the ashes, made off through the woods and were seen no more.

One day we had a deserter among us. I was in a peasant house negotiating for supplies, for soon we would have to

The Sweet Season

take to the woods permanently. Two South Africans came in — Piero and Filippo. Someone wanted to meet me. I walked out with them. At the corner was a German soldier, long-haired, dirty, unarmed. From Hamburg, he said. His family had all been killed in the bombing. He had been on the Russian front. Now he had been drafted to an anti-tank unit below Rome. He was fed up with the war. He wanted to stay with us.

The desire to believe in our fellow men is a strong one. I shook him by the hand and said he could stay. The South Africans took him off to the bivouac we had prepared under a bluff. There we would sit grilling trout and watch the Fascist patrols from Siena come down to the Arbia to our side; they never crossed. The rock face hid the smoke of our fire.

Still we waited for the major to return from Grosseto. The captain and the parachute lieutenant were organizing the peasants. They had been mobilized to cut brushwood for the beacon fires. In the meantime they had to be cheered and encouraged — passionate, slightly cynical men, who measured risks carefully. One evening we all met in a big farmhouse far from the roads to celebrate the prospect of liberation, to keep up morale, to pass the time of waiting. A long table filled the kitchen from hearth to wall. The cloth was thick, home-made linen. The captain sat at the head of the table. I was at his right hand, the men lined both sides. The women began to serve — huge mounds of *pasta asciutta*, boiled meat, boiled tongues, boiled chicken, roast meat, *ricotta*, cheese, and bottle upon bottle of wine. Children gaped at the door, waiting to snatch a half-gnawed bone or a chicken's foot. The cats growled and spat among the debris beneath the table. When the last dish was cleared there was only the wine left. There were speeches from the captain, from myself, from the lieutenant, from the master of the house. Then in turn they sang *stornelli* — the name of a flower followed by a rhyming couplet set to a wavering melodic line. Political, sexual, humorous, obscene, libellous, traditional. Each man sat down to a roar of applause and a chorus shouted in unison:

Pebbles from My Skull

> *Cogli la rosa*
> *e lasc' andar la foglia,*
> *ho tanta voglia*
> *di far con te l'amor.*

The women had gone to eat the remnants in the open and to wash the dirty plates. The stories broadened — stories of peasant cunning, of monstrous practical jokes, of the days when they were conscripts, slept on grass mattresses in the tiered bunks of the grim barracks, and learned to know the brothels of the garrison towns.

Noisily we dispersed through the May night.

On the way back I passed the bivouac. They were all asleep except one South African, older than the others — a gentle man, afraid and not ashamed to admit it. They had been drinking, he said, at a peasant house and the German had got very noisy, shouting and yelling. He didn't like having him about. How did we know who he was? As I walked home I turned the problem over in my mind.

A couple of days later the major was back. There was a council of war in his office. The submarine had been there on time, had put a rubber dinghy ashore. They had told him to listen to London; the signal would be a message: *Le sigarette sono arrivate*. The cigarettes have arrived. The drop would be the same night — after midnight and before three am. We congratulated each other and drank a glass of wine in celebration. I felt a quick, cold stab of fear.

My first task was to alert everyone — the South Africans, Ferruccio, the *carabiniere* cobbler, the peasants I trusted most. My hosts I did not tell — not that I could not trust them, but they were safer in ignorance. The prisoners-of-war were to meet in a stone hut in a meadow by the Arbia in two days' time. The South Africans from the bivouac under the bluff heard my news with a kind of shuffling embarrassment. What about Kurt, they asked, was he to come? I asked what they thought. They were worried, they said. He kept telling them they should all go into Siena to have a good time. He knew the password. Besides he was frighten-

The Sweet Season

ing the peasants. They didn't know what to do. You found him, I said, you can get rid of him. I give you twenty-four hours.

They shot him over breakfast next morning. Filippo was sitting with his tommy-gun by his side. Suddenly, without warning, he lifted it and emptied the magazine. The bullets smashed Kurt's breast. They buried him on the hillside a few yards from the bivouac. There were stones and roots everywhere. It was hard work to get far enough down. In the end there was a little mound. They heaped it over with leaves.

11

A stream marks the eastern limit of Chianti. Beyond its deep valley the land falls in a long reverse slope towards Siena. The mouth of the valley is sealed by a low ridge; from the main road it is impossible to guess at the broad haughs beyond. It would make an admirable dropping zone, easy to pin-point. There was the meeting of the waters where the stream joined the Arbia, just beyond the mouth of the valley. There was the unmistakable triangle of the valley itself — the exact pattern of our beacon fires.

We waited and listened. To rumours of informers trying to penetrate the bands of the Arno valley and the Chianti, of blackmailers extorting money in the name of the partisans. To the radio, searching the wave-bands. German jamming blanketed the voices from London. All day long the monitors were at the sets. The major repeated his instructions. The drop would take place on receipt of the message: *Le sigarette sono arrivate.* Probable time of the drop — midnight to three am.

It was dark early on these May evenings; my family were supping by lamplight when the dog growled beneath the table. There were quick, booted steps in the courtyard. We looked up from the table. I felt the usual start of fright. The door burst open. It was the major.

Carlino, le sigarette sono arrivate.

I was relieved, with a hint of fear left in the pit of my stomach — fear of the dark valley, of the weapons from the air, and the thought of death.

It was a still night, almost cloudless, without moon. By the road to Siena a limekiln flared like a medieval hell. We hoped it might not be mistaken for one of our fires. From

The Sweet Season

far up the valley came the sound of boots on the rocky path. The lieutenant was on his way. I left to inspect the beacons. They were all in place and guarded. In the whispers of the men there was excitement and a hint of nervousness. The gunmen handled their weapons and wiped the dew from the metal. Soon they would have something better in their hands. Once more we checked the signal. Three flashes on a torch. Then they would set the brushwood ablaze. I walked back shivering across the dark hollow of the valley. It was midnight; the sky still; the air cold and damp. Once, far away, we heard the clank of tracks as an armoured column moved down towards the front. A truck roared past the limekiln on the Siena road. An early cock crowed beyond the hills. Then far away we heard a mosquito drone. The whispers ceased. The noise grew, drawing our eyes to the dark spaces between the stars. Somewhere beyond the Milky Way the sound faltered and strayed. In our ears there remained only the pounding of our blood and the resonance of a heartbeat. We waited until the dawn.

The next night and the next again it was the same. With each vigil tension relaxed and prestige was lost. Soon our peasants would begin to waver. The front would jump north. We would hear the guns and nothing done.

At nine-thirty on the fourth night Gino, the young South African, came, his fair hair plastered with sweat. The cigarettes had arrived again. He had warned everyone he could. Together we made for the beacon on the track above the stream and dragged the faggots from among the bushes. Across the valley I heard twigs break; voices floated across the low-lying mist. There was still no sign of the lieutenant and his men; but it would be late before he could collect them from the scattered farms.

Half an hour after midnight and still no sign of the lieutenant. We decided to light the beacons at all costs and run the risk of dawn catching us in the open, gathering the containers. It would be a long task with only two men at my beacon and three at each of the others. Then from the direction of the mill I heard their marching. It was too loud

Pebbles from My Skull

for secrecy. Someone was hurrying ahead. I slid forward the safety catch of my Beretta. It was the lieutenant himself.

Signor capitano, there's one too many.

One what?

A man too many.

Then they came up and I saw him for the first time. A dark figure, small beside his peasant escort. His face was a pale oval against the black mass of the bushes. I was less interested in him than annoyed by the complication.

He can help, can't he?

The lieutenant laughed. He had a way of laughing that was a humourless denial. I moved aside to hear his story. By the mill-pond they had stopped to rest and check for stragglers. The count of heads would not tally. There was one too many. He would not say where he came from. In one pocket they found a blackmail note, scrawled, illiterate, grimy.

Let's have a look at him, I said.

First they searched him, turning out of his pockets tawdry talismans. A St Anthony to guard against the dropped coin and the lost letter; crumpled envelopes scrawled over with addresses; the photograph of a girl with dark hair and staring pin-black eyes. Nothing in his shoes. Nothing in the seams of his clothes. No gun. No money-belt. In his hip-pocket a tattered notebook with addresses in Rome, Volterra, Viterbo, Siena. One in Sardinia. The girl told me nothing with her staring eyes and the scrawled dedication: *Tanti baci dalla Tina*. Then I began to question him.

His first answer was calm and deliberate; the voice, flat, unwavering.

Sono Sardo.

So he came from Sardinia. The man with the torch eased a tired muscle and the circle of light swung a little, leaving the boy's inert hands with their bitten nails to fall full on his face. He blinked and the dark pupils narrowed. What struck me most was the immobility of his features, their apparent lack of depth; a trick of the light perhaps. In that strange

The Sweet Season

blank I could read neither hope nor fear; yet I knew he was frightened from the sudden twitching of his Adam's apple and the uneasy scrabbling of his hands among the leaves.

All the time between the questions and the slow answers, the baffling contradictions, the half-truths and the lies, we listened for a rumour among the stars — a seed of noise that would swell until it filled the valley in the long level dropping run. It was after two. There was an hour left. They would be revving the engines on the runways with the air-screws flickering in the lights. The torch dimmed and came on again. Someone said: 'Put it out, we'll need it later.' I rose to my feet to stretch my cramped legs, lit a cigarette under my jacket, walked a few paces down the path. I heard the lieutenant behind me; he was impatient — almost nervous.

Be', cosa si fa?

What *did* we do?

We turned back. The boy lay on his back by the path, looking up at the dark branches of the trees.

Who wrote these addresses?

I did.

Whose are they?

I don't know.

Why did you write them?

To pass the time, *Dio mio*, to pass the time.

The Siena one too?

Yes, that one too.

He turned his face away. Suddenly he seemed to want only one thing — to be rid of my questions and the beam of the torch in his face. I bent and rolled him on to his back again; the pistol slipped from my pocket. I laid it on my palm and shone the torch on it.

Look, this is no time for jokes. Who are you? Where are you from?

Sono Sardo.

He turned away.

What would you do?

The lieutenant laughed but without humour.

111

Pebbles from My Skull

You decide here.

I had half an hour till dawn to decide. There was still no plane. I felt the argument revolve: it is nearly three, they must carry out the drop soon, he mustn't see it, he must die. Why? Because his story doesn't hold water at any point. That is all, but it is enough.

But still I could not bring out the words.

They had given him a cigarette. He was drawing on it slowly, savouring the harshness of the home-cured tobacco. I had tasted it first in the prison camps. There too I had thought of death. Not that there had been much danger if you discounted over-excited sentries or occasional moments of hysteria when the ranks swayed at roll-call and the guards unslung their rifles. But in the dark there were attacks of childish terror and a cold sweat of fear.

My watch was pale. It was greying for the dawn. They would not come now. But he knew too much. I was sick and angry. Angry that they had failed us, angry with the lieutenant for not helping me to decide, angry with the victim for his existence. At ten to three I turned to the lieutenant.

Bisogna che sparisca.

He's got to disappear. The euphemism of the underground, the secret killers. At first light we split up. The lieutenant and his men dispersed. The South Africans climbed up through the woods with the prisoner to the bivouac. I slept for a couple of hours in a barn. My dreams were shot through with the pulse of engines. It was the plane circling and groping for the dropping zone. At last, beyond the Arbia, under a line of hills, the pilot saw points of flame. He wheeled, levelled out into the dropping run, and the parachutes streamed out over the bivouac fires of a German column.

They shot the boy when I was scrambling across country to see what could be salvaged of the arms drop. It was an instinct of mercy that prompted them to attempt it while he slept, lowering the revolver to the level of his eye. But there was only the click of the pin on the rim of the cartridge. At

The Sweet Season

the noise he woke. They laughed spontaneously, hysterically. *Uno scherzo*, they said, *uno scherzo*. He smiled at the strange jest and turned over to sleep. The second time there was a sharp crack and the smell of singeing as the flash caught his hair. With eyes tight shut he rolled over and said *Madonna*. Then one of them took a carbine and shot him through the forehead.

So I was not there when he died. I felt it as an act of desertion — to him and to the others.

12

What they dropped were Sten guns and ammunition, grenades, boots, socks, cigarettes and chocolates. No light machine-guns. No mortars. Nothing to make us into a real fighting force. Gadgets for sabotage. Little anti-tyre mines. Explosive pencils. Caltrops — whichever way you threw them they landed with a spike in the air. At Bannockburn they stopped the English cavalry. In the deep white dust of the Chianti roads we would lay them for the German supply trucks.

As the containers swung down under their coloured parachutes, the German column had left its breakfast fires and driven off. They took with them three hostages. Good men and old friends. When they were gone the peasants came to break open the cigarette cartons and share out the chocolate. Boots and socks disappeared. The greasy Sten guns in their sacks they left alone. The grenades too and their fuses. It was midday before I could collect a party and get to the spot. The peasants watched us gather the guns. Children came running out the peasant houses with a few cigarettes or a bar of chocolate. They had the same story. There had been a lot more but the others had taken it all. I let them keep what they had, accepting the lie. They were being paid at last for months of hospitality and trust.

From that day on the pattern of life was splintered. At dusk the road over the bridge to Siena was full of traffic: trucks with riflemen on the running boards and another erect behind the driving cab; little horse-drawn carts; droves of looted cattle and oxen; men on foot in German uniform, armed and unarmed; deserters; Russians and Poles from the Organization Todt, pressed into service as auxiliaries and

The Sweet Season

now deserting in groups. German reconnaissance planes came buzzing up the valleys, looking for gun positions in the hills to cover the retreat to Florence. The men of my family watched it all calmly as they walked between the vines and sprayed them with copper sulphate. The green fluid ran over their shirts, their faces, their hands. Up and down they went, with a clank of the handle as they pumped the spray. On the vine leaves the fluid pearled and dried into a grey-green bloom. The wheat was ripe for cutting. The fireflies were gone. The binder was ordered from their cousins over the hill. Then one morning we woke to find the wheat by the roadside trampled and eaten by passing baggage trains. That evening I got the grandmother and talked to her for hours by the fire. They were too near the road. One day the Germans would come up the cart-track and stop at the farmhouse. They would kill her rabbits, her hens and her chickens. They would drive off the oxen. They would take everything they could take. What they couldn't take they would smash. So the family must leave and go over the hill to their cousins. Lock, stock and barrel. Next day she gave the order. In slow cartloads they moved their belongings and the farmhouse was left empty. Two days later the Germans came. From that day on the house was seldom without them.

I slept now in a hut of broom in a thick plantation on the edge of the major's estate or slipped into barns as in my wandering days. The cross-country paths were still safe but in the farmyards the men in field-grey were foraging. The prisoners-of-war had to be kept together for night operations — the laying of mines, the cutting of telephone poles to lay ambushes across lonely roads as far as possible from peasant houses and the fear of reprisals. Held together, too, for the time when they would have to be brought through the line. Tempers were shortening and once, after midnight, two of the South Africans fought — Filippo the boxer, and his friend Piero, who first had found me. They sparred at each other for a few minutes. Filippo had an enormous reach. Suddenly Piero drew a knife. We caught

Pebbles from My Skull

his arm and twisted it from his hand. He cursed in Afrikaans and vaulting a gate went off through the night. It was Kurt's knife, taken off his dead body.

We stripped the oil from the Stens and filled the magazines. I primed the grenades and taught the Italians how to throw them. We practised with a couple far up the valley. The explosions rang over the mill pond. As the front came nearer our numbers grew. There was a group of Poles — boys in their teens, wild and uncontrollable, eager to kill. There were political refugees from Siena — a painter, one of them, tall and handsome; his nickname — Caravaggio. He was my liaison officer and moved far and wide over the country, checking on troop movements, getting food for the Poles, for ourselves, for the Jewish architect hiding now in the woods with his family. Coming on a solitary German truck he jumped on the running board and disarmed the driver and his mate. Then back he came across country with a couple of rifles and a Mauser. But these were not enough for our band or for the *levée en masse* of which the major dreamt, as in his green knickerbocker suit he walked his estate and cheered his peasants. On each house he had set the badge of his family — three roses — a rebus on his family name. He was afraid of nothing that the front might bring but looked forward to it with a sort of tremulous excitement. What he feared was the backwash of the war — social disruption, the old ways destroyed, the peasants caught in politics and the class struggle shifted from town to country.

It was he who first came on the ammunition lorry. Walking through the woods he saw it parked at the edge of the trees. There was a little bivouac tent in the shade of a thicket of briars. He strolled past, bade good day to a couple of Germans sunbathing on the grass, and, as he came by the end of the lorry, spotted under its tarpaulins stacked boxes of ammunition. There had been two more, the peasants said. The others had driven away but this one wouldn't start. A sergeant or some sort of NCO had gone off to Siena for a spare part.

We attacked on a hot June day. The woods were heavy

The Sweet Season

with sunshine. Beetles came drifting over the bushes like bombers. There were six of us — the major, myself, four South Africans. We came to the edge of the wood and saw the bivouac tent a couple of hundred yards away across an open field of grass. There was no movement. They would be asleep in the shade or in the back of the truck. We climbed a fence and jumped down among the trailing branches of a briar. A thorn whipped back and struck a South African in the eye ball. He dropped his Sten and clapped a hand to his eye. There was a report as the jolt of the fall brought the firing pin forward on to the cartridge. At the edge of the wood a couple of figures in bathing trunks rose and peered across through the sunshine. We ran forward with a shout. They had their hands up — boys caught in a wave of fear that melted their guts and loosened their sphincters. I looked for the other two. One was by the truck in a little nest of branches he had made for shelter from the sun. He was scrabbling for a weapon. I shouted in German not to be a fool. He stood up with a grenade in his hand and tugged at the thong which would arm the fuse. When I fired he was a couple of yards away. Two shots from the Beretta. One after the other. I saw two little marks appear on his belly, just above his bathing trunks. He clapped his hands over them and fell on his back. You idiot, I said, and bent over him. His face blenched under the sunburn. He groaned a little and twisted about as if to shake off his death. Then he half sat up, looked at my face, and seized my hand, clinging to it like a frightened child. I laid him back and freed myself from his grasp. My hand was sticky with his blood. Beyond the woods the fourth of them was running through the fields, doubling and ducking. At that range there was no point in trying to catch him or to bring him down.

In the truck we found small-arms ammunition — the wrong calibre — mortar bombs, and newfangled anti-tank weapons we didn't know how to use. The wounded man lay in the shade and groaned.

We made the other two carry him and set off through the woods. In a safe spot we rested and waited for evening. He was silent now, his face a strange ashen hue. There was no haemorrhage, only a little dark blood oozing from the two holes. The flesh had closed again over the bullets. We covered him with a blanket and got water to bathe the sweat from his face. His mates sat together and watched and did not talk. After dusk a peasant cart came with a mattress and jolted him along the tracks to the nearest farmhouse. We laid him in the barn in the straw and covered him well. From time to time he would open his eyes and look at me with incredulity. A fair-haired boy with a good face lying in the mucky sweat of death.

When I went in the others were all round the table eating supper. I spoke with the boys and told them not to be afraid. Unless they did anything stupid they were safe. A doctor was coming for the one outside.

He came towards midnight, looked, felt his pulse, shrugged. There's not much to be done about it, he said. I'll give him an injection for his heart. He may last the night. Even if you got him to a hospital there's not much hope.

A South African came and stood beside us.

What does he say?

He says there's not much hope. Maybe we could leave him by the roadside tomorrow with a note. There's bound to be a convoy.

The boy stirred, opened his eyes and looked up at me in the light of the lantern.

Will I die? he asked in English. Will I die?

I told him what we would do. He shut his eyes and slept.

In the morning he was worse; his breathing was laboured and irregular. Caravaggio came to report that parachutists had been dropped to us — Italian saboteurs from Bari. I took a last look at the boy and went off through the woods. I had gone about a mile when from the direction of the farmhouse I heard three bursts of fire.

They are buried on the major's estate in the midst of the high broom. The peasant who kept the stud bull showed me the spot,

The Sweet Season

leading me down through the bushes with an air of mystery. We came to a little open patch. The broom was high above our heads. The air was full of the rumour of insects. He planted his heel in the turf. 'They're here,' he said. 'Who?' I asked. 'The three Germans.' The air between the bushes was hot, still and aromatic. 'Poor things,' I said, using the Italian formula, 'They too were sons of mothers.' 'What do you mean "poor things",' he said. 'We didn't kill enough of them.'

13

One morning I stood in the stubble of a wheat field and watched my family reap the last sheaves of grain. Dino jumped from the seat of the ox-drawn binder, wiped the sweat from his face, and asked for a glass of water. His brothers filled it with clear, colourless *grappa* and roared with laughter as its fire caught at the back of his dry throat. I did not see them again.

Now it was difficult to move except in the very heart of the woods. Caravaggio was shot dead on a dusty road as he stepped out from the bushes to hold up a lorry. The bullet struck between the eyes. The lieutenant took a party over the hills and ambushed a column of troops. He came back swinging a German helmet and complaining that British hand grenades were no good. If there hadn't been so many duds they would have killed the lot. He reported to me where I lay in bed in a peasant house with dysentery and fever. (We each have our peculiar defences against the difficult moments of life.) That night the Germans burned every house within a couple of miles of the ambush and killed the menfolk.

The Poles had captured a German lorry and drove about exchanging shots with German columns. Driving up to a rendezvous in their field-grey uniforms, they would jump down shouting *Alle 'raus*. They thought it immensely funny. In the dark friend and foe looked alike. Going to visit the *cantiniere* at Brolio we found a Volkswagen truck parked outside his house. There was nothing worth taking in the pockets or under the dashboard. In the morning the truck had gone.

There was no time now for zither lessons but once with the parachute lieutenant I visited the widower and his daughter to get supplies for the Poles — flour, wine and some eggs. I found them jumpy. They had had Germans in

The Sweet Season

the house all night; another party had arrived and was eating supper. We stood at the foot of a six-foot bank, hidden by a barn and whispered. From along the road came a steady tramping noise. Scrambling up the grass I could see two men with rifles. They were talking loudly, drunkenly. They would pass along the road just above our heads. As they drew near they were quiet except for an occasional laugh. Their steps came past the barn. Suddenly they were charging down the slope. As I raised my pistol I recognized Filippo and his mate, Piero. We cursed each other in whispers. They were drunk, giggling and noisy. I told them to shut up and went on talking to the *fattore*. As we arranged for an ox-cart to deliver the provisions I was aware of the pair whispering and sniggering together behind me. Then came an unmistakable noise — a rifle bolt driving the bullet into the breech. No one spoke — neither the South Africans, nor the lieutenant by my side, nor the *fattore*, the little dark man facing me with his back to the barn. I made an effort and went on with the details — when I could expect delivery? How would the Poles recognize the peasant driving the oxen? How much I must promise to pay in the name of the partisans? The two men with the guns began to whisper together, moved aside a little and argued. The lieutenant shifted his stance and turned to cover them with his revolver. Suddenly, without explanation, the pair shouldered their rifles, turned and walked away.

From that day we heard of them only at second hand. How they raided the German bivouacs and drove off the looted cattle to sell to the black-market butchers; the profits went on a cache of drink. How up on the edge of Chianti they sacked the house of a local Fascist — a harmless creature who gladly let himself be blackmailed into silence and months before, as a token of goodwill, had had the pair to supper. They had spoken glowingly of his wine and his daughter. Now he was in hiding, waiting for the front to pass. In the empty house they broke what they could, ate and drank, rummaged in the girl's bedroom, wading among the scattered underwear, crunching the broken

Pebbles from My Skull

mirrors underfoot. Before leaving, they fouled the staircase. Looters, if they could, would smear the whole world with their excrement.

Walking with one of our parachutists — a fearless little man from Bari — I turned the corner of a farmyard and came on a German boy eating a hunk of bread. His long rifle lay by his side. We passed the time of day and walked on. By chance we were both unarmed. A hundred yards beyond the farm the Italian laid his hand on my arm and said: Wait here. I watched him walk back the way we had come, then I sat by the path and waited. He was a long time away. When he came, he had the rifle in his hand. What did you do to him? I asked. Nothing, he replied, I explained that there are a lot of partisans about and that he'd be safer without this thing. Then I put him in the barn and shut the door.

We took him out at night. He was a miserable, frightened child, straggler or deserter, lost and hungry. We gave him food and took him blindfold into the woods, spun him round three times, and pushed him off. He stood still for a minute fumbling at the bandage on his eyes, waiting perhaps for the bullet to strike between his shoulders. Then he stumbled forward and began to run into the dark.

One clear morning the sky was filled with noise and out of the south there came a multitude of aircraft, very steady, very high, trailing threads of condensation. The noise of their engines beat down from the sky and filled the whole landscape. The shadows passed over plain and valleys, over the Arbia, over the hills of Chianti. They disappeared at last beyond the Apennines and the drumming of the motors followed them.

On the radio the names in the communiques were now familiar — Radiocofani, Val d'Orcia, Val di Chiana. In his ancestral home the major laid out his uniform. From Siena came word that we should wear tricolour cockades if we wished to avoid summary execution as *franctireurs* and orders that I was to go into Siena and act as liaison officer when the town fell to the Allies.

It was a hot, close, moist day when I set off with the

The Sweet Season

young student who had brought me my identity card. But for a photograph it was complete in all details. Over the signature of the Fascist mayor it stated that I, Luigi Neri, was a member of the auxiliary police and had the right to carry arms. From the major I had a suit, a silk shirt and tie, shoes and a raincoat. The pockets were stuffed with explosives to be delivered in Siena. In soft rain we walked down towards the town, past the spot where the truck had stood and the German boys had camped under the thorn bushes. Soon we were in unfamiliar country with the town rising high above us on its hills. Outside the gates there was a signpost bristling with German unit signs; on the gate, a German sentry. As we walked towards him I felt once more, as when I was a child, caught and about to be beaten, sweat breaking at the base of my spine. The sentry hunched under his camouflaged cape and watched us pass. The instinct to run was strong. We walked on up the steep pavements and the houses rose on either side. At the first barber's shop I had my hair cut; in the photographer's next door, my picture taken. That night I slept in a flat off the Via Montanini. My bedroom window was set at the end of a little courtyard. On one side was the church of Sant'Andrea. Under the eaves of the church was a stone head weathered to a grotesque, hare-lipped mask.

There are no sculptures on the church of Sant'Andrea; I have looked. Yet I know this mask intimately and can recall it at will. Perhaps my window looked out on some other part of the church; perhaps the nightmare face is a projection of my fears.

It was strange to be in a town again, to move among people, to see shops, even if the windows were half-empty. The conduit bringing the town's water supply from the Monte Amiata had been cut; night and morning the townsfolk went down the steep alleys to the Fontebranda, under the house of St Catharine, to draw water from the ancient

Pebbles from My Skull

wells. I took my turn to go down with the pitchers, walking unnoticed among them, listening to their rumours, hopes and fears. On my arm was the brassard of the auxiliary police. I had reported to my contact, a good-natured Sicilian colonel. I found him at about ten in the morning still in his pyjamas. We had a cup of barley coffee together. He dressed and proposed a walk through the town. As we stepped out on to the steep flagged street, two men rose out of doorways further up the hill; two more came out of alleyways behind us. My gunmen, said the colonel. The same men as were daily working through a list of collaborators and informers. The killings left dark bloodstains on the pavements. Within their protective box we moved through the town. I learned about the seventeen *contrade* and the ritual of the *palio*. I must come back one day and see it, said the colonel, it was worth the journey. At the end of our promenade we shook hands. He knew, he said, where to get me if necessary.

So I was on holiday and spent my days exploring, getting the feel of the town, succumbing occasionally to claustrophobia between the high houses, happiest in the Piazza del Campo, where the shadow of the campanile swept the hours away like a huge sundial, or in the Piazza del Duomo under the black and white bell-tower of the cathedral. Here one day a German truck drew up behind me and a detail of troops jumped down. I stood on the steps of the cathedral and wondered whether to stay. With an officer at their head they came up the steps in a little bunch. There was something informal about the way they moved — a lack of military precision. On the mosaiced terrace, beneath the triple doorway, they halted, grouped themselves round the officer and listened — as I did — edging my way towards them as he told of the great plan to build a church to rival Florence's Santa Maria del Fiore and how it failed. In the distance there was the grumbling noise of battle.

Once, in the streets, real fear took me. It was midday and the narrow ways were thronged. Suddenly the cry went up that the Germans had sealed the street and were rounding up

The Sweet Season

the able-bodied men. The pavements emptied. From near the great square of the *palio* came shouts and cries. I turned into a church. A bell tinkle for the elevation of the host. I knelt among the old women, watching their movements and gestures. The priest came and went before the altar. There was a tingling smell of incense. When mass was over I walked out. The streets were filling again. The guns had moved nearer.

The front was close. Behind the town were German batteries. Day and night their shells curved high over the Torre del Mangia and the chequered façade of the Duomo. In reply came the sighing, whispering salvoes of the Allied counter-battery fire; they burst somewhere beyond the walls. At night I lay in bed in terror and heard them pass overhead. Worse still was a single plane, unexplained, unidentified, which buzzed over the town for hours on end like a lazy mosquito. I lay and followed its slow, meandering flight, to and fro, over and back. Suddenly there would be an explosion and a tinkle of broken glass. Allied or German, it was incomprehensible, a communal nightmare, the source of speculation and wild rumour when the queues formed next day at the Fontebranda.

One morning, before dawn, there was a scuffling noise of feet in the street. I looked out and saw the German rearguards falling back through the town, deliberate, unhurrying, dragging their light anti-tank guns behind them. For half an hour or more, the town lay in the greying light, silent and empty. Quiet figures in long grey cloaks began to slip along the walls. They were almost indistinguishable from those that had preceded them. The same even pace, the same concentration. They were in single file with rifles at the ready. The town woke and came out into the streets to greet the liberators. The *Goumiers* turned their alert wild faces to the applauding crowds and passed quickly on with the intent, withdrawn look of men going into action, out through the gates, and up into the foothills of Chianti. The crowds thickened in the streets. The bell of the Torre del Mangia began to peal as it does at great moments in the life

Pebbles from My Skull

of Siena. There were troops everywhere. Officers in pale blue kepis, officers in long, dashing cloaks. Still the people clapped and shouted as the troops filed past under the walls of the high palaces. In front of me one French officer turned to another and said, looking at the holiday faces of the crowd: *Ils le regretteront*.

I went off to seek out the colonel. The French had taken over the Excelsior Hotel up by the *place d' armes*. We reported to the divisional chief of staff, told him about bridges, gun positions, roads, paths. He was busy, curt, and incurious. At midday the major came through the lines. The Germans were holding the foothills with a screen of rearguards. He stayed for lunch at the Excelsior. There were toasts and speeches. Outside the town was on holiday. The Poles came marching in wearing their German uniforms; at their head was a boy on a mule brandishing a rifle. They had the South Africans with them and two saboteurs. The others had been killed in the Allied shell-fire as they came through the vineyards. Feruccio was there saying I must come to the Questura and explain that the police were Fascists. In an inner office, a couple of British officers with strange shoulder tabs looked at me dubiously and said they had to work with whoever was available. The major had disappeared again. The colonel was nowhere to be found. In the Piazza del Campo a French military band was playing shrilly with a clash of cymbals, marching and counter-marching. The men of the *contrade* appeared in costume and paraded round the great square. They tossed their flags high up towards the unattainable bells. There was gunfire in the plains. Six, seven miles away, in the woods of Chianti, the patrols probed and clashed.

Up in the wooded hills, the colonel was guiding an armoured patrol through his estate, riding with the leading tank. There was a sudden sharp clash with the German rearguards. On his own ground he redeemed his honour with a flesh wound. Passed back along the line from first aid post to advanced dressing-station,

The Sweet Season

sucked into the flow of sick, wounded and mutilated, he came to his senses somewhere near Tripoli in North Africa. He was being carried from a transport plane. Apart from bandages, he did not have a stitch of clothing. His peaked cap, olive-green, gold-braided, covered his nakedness.

I wandered on through the city. From a window in the Communist Party headquarters Feruccio grinned and beckoned me over. I must stop the disarming of the partisans. I contrived to escape. On the public buildings they were busy with paint and chisels defacing the symbols of tyranny. A South African said there was a truck going back to base, wherever that might be. Half a dozen of us collected, climbed over the tail-board and drove off. We were out of place in a world of uniforms. We had stood still in time and did not know it.

The first staging-point was a French prisoner-of-war cage. They put us in beside the Germans. I sat on the grass and was dumb with fury and reaction. That evening an American truck picked us up. We drove all night over mountain passes and through ruined towns. The dust of the bombardments swirled up over the tailboard. It was bitterly cold. In the morning there was Civitavecchia, crumbling and destroyed, American rations, ice cream, white bread, strange, sloppy troops. Before sunset we boarded a tank-landing-craft. I was not to leave the ship, I was told; must consider myself more or less under arrest. There were two berths in my cabin. Someone woke up in the lower one and switched on the light. A priest. I greeted him. He smiled and did not immediately answer. Haltingly he explained that he was German. I answered in his own tongue and he relaxed. The vessel cast off. Soon we could feel the slap of her flat bows on the waves. He told me his story. Called to attend the execution of a young deserter he had comforted the boy, saying: *Du stirbst für die gute Sache.* You are dying in a good cause. Then he had himself deserted, found shelter in the Vatican, and now was on his way, a volunteer, to serve

Pebbles from My Skull

in the prison camps of the Middle East.

A sailor looked in and said food was ready. The priest shook his head and took up his prayer book. I went off after the sailor. In the little wardroom I found the captain — a small, emphatic, bearded Greek. He would have no Germans at his table, he said. Had I been in uniform I would, I suppose, have agreed mutely, drunk my tot of gin and sat down. But I had been too long on my own, forming my own judgments. In that case, I said, I would prefer to wait and eat after the others, along with the priest.

From that moment the two of us were together. In a grey dawn we watched Ischia and Capri go past. There was a smirr of rain over the water. We had talked far into the night, discussing guilt and how one lived with it, debating whether original sin were the same as the dark forces we repress within us, whether punishment was absolute or whether judgment should be conditional on understanding of motive. I remembered the flaccid pietism of my boyhood Sundays and contrasted it with this man's arguments in which Freud and Jung reinforced theology. I told him of the deaths I had on my conscience and the difficulty of decision when all points of reference are gone. I explained the candid naive illusions of my youth, the absolute trust in human decency with which I had gone to war, the difficulty of preserving some balance between cynicism and despair on the one hand, hope on the other. You must not, he said, despair of men — your Italian peasants speak against it — but you must be prepared for disappointment, not expect too much, and accept goodness, when you meet it, as a manifestation of grace. By evening we had skirted along the Costa Amalfitana and were near Salerno. There were trucks waiting on the quay. We shook hands under the eye of the Greek captain and parted. He came from the abbey of Fulda. A man of medium height, round-headed, dark-haired, a Rhinelander. I owe him a great debt.

14

From Salerno to Naples is just over thirty miles by road. I remember none of it. I remember, from the back of a truck, seeing above Naples an American military prison compound. Men of all colours walked up and down, played games or hung on the wire-netting and looked out. At an Italian barracks by the sea at the foot of Vesuvius I came back into the world. My Italian suit I gave to a corporal in stores, my Italian shoes and my Italian silk shirt. The shirt he fingered professionally. I said I wanted it back. Sir, he explained, they must all be disinfected. I knew I would never see it again. Like a raw recruit I came out again with army boots in my hand, a pile of kit on my arm and stupid questions in my head. Where could I get my regimental cap badge? Would they have tartan flashes in Naples? In the barrack-room I found some old faces. They called out with the easy, meaningless camaraderie of war, asking for news of Tom and Dick and Harry. In this communal world of the dormitory they were at home, organized, snug. In their public schools they had been trained for just such a life with the same food, the same rags. For them the rules and restrictions in barracks or prisoner-of-war camp were familiar, breeding nostalgia. But here there were aliens to break the easy routine. Yugoslavs, first of all, officers of the Royal Yugoslav army in strange greenish uniforms and an excess of braid. I should watch the little old captain, they told me. He got pissed on a bottle of wine every night and walked about starkers in a sheet. The Holy Ghost, they called him. And in a small dormitory, by themselves, the Russians. A dozen Red Army officers who had joined the Todt Organization and worked for the Germans. I spoke to

Pebbles from My Skull

them. They crowded round, asking for help, asking me to live in their room and treat with the world that held them prisoner. From them I first heard of the great camps where the Russians died of hunger and disease, of dead bodies kept in the bunks and slowly eaten, now a liver, now a heart, of the German camera teams filming the starving men rushing a field kitchen for some thin soup, of the choice between that and technical collaboration. They had been used as drivers, mostly, bringing up supplies; amateurs of petty sabotage, they laughed at the solemn rigidity of the German mind and the ease with which they could trick it. They had deserted and fought with the partisans. What would happen when they got home? I asked. A young dark man, bent over his balalaika, looked up and said: *Rasstrel*. Firing squad.

For three weeks I lived with them. I was screened by security and passed the test. I told them what I knew about the great line building above Migliana. I was vaccinated, inoculated, re-fitted. I bathed on a beach of dark sand — lava or coal; tiny bits of pumice stone bobbed on the water amidst the Neapolitan sewage. The transports lay out in the bay. At night the searchlights leapt up. There was gunfire. The Allies were held beyond Florence. I thought of war pushing up through the mountains. In the San Carlo I saw *Madam Butterfly*. There was an officers' club in a big house. Someone got into a suit of armour and couldn't get out. There was warm rain.

At night I talked to my neighbour — a Georgian captain. Before the war he had worked in films with Eisenstein. His wife was a doctor. Under the Germans he had volunteered as orderly in a field hospital; he had found himself doing operations. When he left his wife said: If I do not hear from you for two years I shall shoot myself. It was now three years since he said goodbye. We went to the cinema together — an inexplicable American thriller with long sequences missing. We played chess. He warned me against the man in the opposite corner — a man from the steppes, a Kalmuck, who would preach at me for hours, quoting the Short History of the Communist Party of the Soviet Union.

The Sweet Season

They did not trust him, said the captain. He talked too much. I should pay no attention.

In the early morning I was wakened from my sleep. Would I come to the guardroom. There was a wounded Russian lying on a blanket on the floor with half his head blown off. His eyes were open. Ask his name, said the orderly officer, and who did it. I tried. There was no reply. I asked again. The mouth opened and groaned. The eyes became vacant. I went back to bed.

Next day the Kalmuck had disappeared. The military police picked him up within twenty-four hours. There was a Mauser in the box beneath his bed. Under his armpit he bore the stencilled blood group of the SS. A Soviet colonel came down, broad-shouldered and jovial. He drank pink gins in the mess and said he would deal with the matter. We shall send them all home soon, he added. One afternoon I came back from Naples and the room was empty.

Pompeii. Touts selling test-tubes of volcanic ash; beggars hawking flowers; a queue at the lupanar. Priapus, chrysophallic at the door, was unveiled to US top sergeants and giggling girls in uniform. In each cubicle, above the stone couch, was pictured the sad monotony of the sexual act.

The steamer was high and grey. We walked up the gangway. Boat-drill: Cheap gin. The Atlas Mountains, The Sierra Nevada. The escort carrier pitching and rolling like a surrealist billiard-table. A kind of limbo in which I discovered that I had lost the knack of looking beyond tomorrow. A burial at sea. Two days out from Liverpool — soldier, sailor, tinker, tailor — he died on his way home. The ship rocks quietly. The corvettes circle. The plank tilts. The body hesitates above the waves, slips and is gone.

Landfall with Blackpool tower just above the horizon. Four years before it had been my last sight of England.

Epilogue

What I have to try to explain is this: Why did it take me from 8 September 1943 to 15 August 1944 to cross the line, reassume my identity, step back out of limbo? There are half a dozen excuses ready to hand — ignorance, mistaken judgments, bad luck, the slowness of the Allied advance, the weather, the terrain. I was doing something for the war effort. I had a responsibility for the escaped prisoners who turned to me for guidance. I had a moral obligation to the major and his group. All this is true and irrelevant. What kept me in limbo was that I did not want to emerge from it.

In part I was caught by a regression in time. Living with the peasants I saw the last upsurge of peasant life and of an ancient civilization — *la civiltà contadinesca*. The skills I learned, the crafts I watched, had not changed since Ambrogio Lorenzetti in the fourteenth century painted his great murals in the Town Hall of Siena. War, blockade, economic autarchy, had cancelled out such small progress as the last fifty years had seen. Trade had ceased, except for an occasional pedlar with a pack of thread, needles, pins and almanacs. Each family lived to itself and for itself, spinning its own wool, making its own tools, providing its own food. When Dino went out in March to prune his vines with his broad-bladed knife or stopped to hone his scythe on the verge of the farm track, he had the exact gestures and rhythms of a peasant from Breughel or some Book of the Hours. He waited for spring with the same longing as they did, looking beyond the cold and misery of winter to the days when the sun took courage and birds courted. Like them he let war pass over him and kept his thoughts on the next harvest, which was more important than who won. I

Epilogue

saw his courage and suffering, his joys and festivals. I learned that time can be accepted with the passing of the seasons, that birth, life and death can be seen calmly as part of a great rhythm of blossom and decay.

Today the brides no longer bring a dowry of chestnut-trees. The girls no longer wear the coarse homespun stockings. The women no longer fan the little charcoal stoves. They have methane gas and are the better for it. The young men cavort on their motor-scooters and the girls sit side-saddle, flouncing their nylon petticoats. I am glad — and glad that I saw what went before.

In part I was merely taking time out of life — escaping from war, which is itself an escape from reality. That is why, with one part of their being, men and women welcome it, for its promise of freedom, sexual and otherwise, for its lifting of taboos. In society we build up strong sanctions. You may not smash windows, nor walk into houses, nor (decently) read other people's letters. In wartime the censorship is full of unrepressed Paul Prys. The gunners smash with a single round all the virgin windows of their youth. The infantry break down all the doors ever shut against them, sleep in forbidden beds, rake through drawers, cupboards, chests. Even this was not enough for me. I had to escape from the reality of war into something more romantic. A fugue within a fugue.

In the last analysis, I dawdled because I liked it. There are moments in our lives when outward circumstances so exactly correspond to the inner structure of our being that our actions acquire an uncanny certainty. Some are lucky enough to be born into this state of 'correspondence'. They are fish in water. Their thoughts, judgments and actions, have a sureness that owes nothing either to intelligence or cunning. To others this ease in living comes only spasmodically, in particular circumstances and for a brief time. Perhaps this conjunction gave the months I spent in Chianti their peculiar quality of happiness, overriding fear and the need to kill.

In 1943 I was 'not shy but incredibly reserved'. Reserve

Pebbles from My Skull

was my defence against the world. I had worked on it for years — ever since, as a child, I had learned to protect myself from emotional pressures, loving inquisitions, the prying and surveillance that went with coddled ill-health. Freedom lay in withdrawal or escape over the garden wall and beyond the reach of calling voices. Lying in the bracken or the fronded, hollow-stemmed herbs by the river, I looked up at the clouds as they passed between the tree-tops with a squeamish motion and was hidden and protected. I had few friends then and few later. Most of them were fellow-conspirators. Our enemy was no longer the petty tyranny of the family but the authority of a hierarchical society. Now and again the luck of war threw a couple of us together in an army training-school, on a staff, in a transit camp. We recognized each other by an intonation, a silence when others laughed, a glancing reference, the avoidance of certain words. These chance meetings were scattered among a desert of non-committal acquaintance. Yet there was nothing I wished more than to be drawn into a fuller community. It was a desire I came to link more and more with one memory. An evening lit with the peacock hues of the north. We had been playing on the sands, running and tumbling together — two brothers, their sister and myself. On the shifting dunes she caught me by the hand and ran down the long unmarred slope. The sun had reached its northern limit beyond the hills. The wind twitched the cold sand and stung our legs. Their mother appeared to send them to bed. She kissed them one by one. I stood apart and watched. In my family we did not kiss so easily. 'Will I kiss you, too?' she asked, coming towards me so that I saw the pale dusting of powder on her cheek. Then I was caught between the sweep of the bay and the dunes in a great circle of love.

The journey from Migliana across the Sieve and the Arno had been a nightmare of despair and loneliness. Each evening as I came up to knock at a farm door I was seized by terror of rejection. Daily my predicament touched off fears that went back to the earliest moments of my life. In

Epilogue

Chianti, after a period of absolute exclusion, I became one of a family and of a conspiracy. Beside the Arbia, in the moist woods, and in the dry scrub of the hillsides I lay and felt the old security. A mole came burrowing up through the grass at my side, the jays swung on the branches overhead, and the snakes swished and glinted through last year's leaves. I walked in safety through dark tunnels among the broom and felt the night protect me. The currents of my life flowed together and swept me along. I wish their stream might have been more productive of human good, less costly in lives.

We get little help from others in living. What we learn from them are mostly the inessentials of life — tricks and skills. But occasionally we exchange obscure signals. They are reassurances that others face or have faced the same difficulties, problems, choices. That they react to the same stimuli, feel the same joy and anguish, make the same sort of shifts to deal with foreknowledge of mortality. We may record the past for various reasons: because we find it interesting; because by setting it down we can deal with it more easily; because we wish to escape from the prison where we face our individual problems, wrestle with our particular temptations, triumph in solitude and in solitude accept defeat and death. Autobiography is an attempted jail-break. The reader tunnels through the same dark.

Afterword

The true picture of the past flits by, wrote Walter Benjamin, and 'can be seized only as an image which flashes up at the instant when it can be recognized and is never seen again'. There is a sense in which for me that instant occurred in 1963, when this account of my time in Italy was first put down on paper. I had tried to seize it once before, soon after my return to Britain, but I abandoned the effort, for all I was capable of producing was a chronicle of events, places, dates, to which I could ascribe no meaning, give no coherence. Nor, although the events of 1943 were closer then, did I remember them with the same apparent accuracy and clarity as informed my later effort, which was an attempt to come to terms with an important experience in the light of what the Italians call *il senno del poi*, the wisdom that derives from distance in time: the distance which, as Benjamin has it, the angel of history puts behind him as, with his face turned towards the past, he is irresistibly propelled into the future. Having once identified and fixed the image (with all its blemishes and inaccuracies) I have been able to reflect on it, consider it, and to acquire a better understanding of some events and some experiences. I have, for instance, learned from others details of my own behaviour which have surprised me. Thus in one account of the days following our liberation from prisoner-of-war camp — an account I have no reason to disbelieve — I learn that I returned to the village in which we had been confined, along with one of the Italian staff, to see whether the Germans were still in occupation. Of this there is no trace in my memory, my version. Nor is there of a moment described by Ted, my companion for the first months of liberty. It concerns an evening which I recalled, as it seemed to me with total clarity. Emerging on to a main road we found ourselves in the midst of a group of German soldiers

Afterword

walking in the same direction as ourselves. As we walked along, he tells me, he asked: 'What do we do now?' To which, it seems, I replied: 'Pay no attention to them.' Shortly afterwards a path allowed us to leave the road and their company. It is as if I were hearing a report about some stranger.

On other important matters, too, I have had to consider new perspectives. These were in part a natural result of the passage of time, of reflection on my part on such topics as the war, on politics, on the nature of the Resistance and the way in which it had become over the years central to the ideology of the Italian Communist Party: a legend which may not be challenged, which justifies any political turn, and participation in which rebuts all possibility of criticism. In little Italian towns the large black-edged posters announcing the death of some member of the Garibaldi brigades demonstrate the degree to which these old men have been absorbed into a hagiography of the Left, which has always inclined to a cult of martyrs and of the dead. I first understood something of this when I was asked to form part of a delegation from Britain to a congress of ANPI, the Communist-dominated partisan association. Speaking to the assembly from a platform on which were seated Communist Party officials, Yugoslav functionaries and Soviet generals, and listening in turn to their speeches, I learned to what extent the courage and sacrifices of the men and women I had known in Tuscany had become the object of ritual admiration, celebrated with a rhetoric which aimed to use their history to justify the present-day shifts of Party policy.

What also gave a new focus to my perceptions was a sociological theory concerning the attitude of Italian peasants to escaped prisoners of war like myself. Briefly the theory is that in an escaped prisoner the peasants saw both an object of immense value, which conveyed prestige in the community to its possessors (although possession was not without its dangers) and a pledge which might be exchanged profitably in terms of cash or goodwill, or both,

Pebbles from My Skull

when at last the Allies arrived: an insurance policy if you like. It is a theory which tends to exclude the element of human compassion and to declare the predominance in the peasant's mind of calculation: an equation which I do not find altogether acceptable. Thus the value I represented may account for some of the distress felt by the family that sheltered me, when I left abruptly during a Fascist raid; but I am convinced that, on another level, it sprang from genuine human concern over my fate. For I believe that the motives of human action are highly complex and allow for the coexistence of contradictory motives and sentiments; we are impaled very often on the contradictions inherent in our society and specific moments in its history. Yet that there were some solid grounds for the theory I learned from Maurilio, the man who, as a partisan liaison officer, had found a family to accept me.

In the summer of 1981 I returned to the village above Prato where I had found shelter in January and February 1944. It was, in fact, the fourth time I had returned, although one visit hardly counted since I had done no more than look at the village from a spot where I had seen the Fascist militia debus and form up in a line to attack uphill towards a partisan position. There we picnicked and made love before driving into the village, which was well on its way to becoming a holiday resort, full of second homes, with the scars of war (such as they were) deleted. What signalled the change was not so much the fact that the house which an American tank had damaged had been demolished as the disappearance of the spring gushing from the wall under the house that had been my refuge — the spring from which even in winter the women had used to get their water in copper jugs. What brought me back to the village in 1981 was the extraordinary coincidence that here an English sociologist and a sociologist from the University of Florence were examining the theory I have outlined above. The English sociologist knew of me from having read (in Washington) my debriefing — the account of my wanderings I had given to military intelligence in Naples as I waited for repatriation

Afterword

— and knew too from fieldwork my friends and acquaintances in the village. He had warned me that there were two schools of thought in the community: those who maintained that 'Carlino' was a legend and the others who insisted they had known him, that he had indeed existed. My visit in 1981 would therefore be for some in the nature of an epiphany. This was less important than the fact that I learned from him that Franco was there. On two visits after the war I had been unable to find him or indeed to gather any very concrete intelligence about his history. People were evasive about him, giving vague indications that he was in Prato somewhere and had a shop selling gas appliances, or else that he travelled as a salesman in that line. This time I found him in a new house at the far end of the village. When I knocked on the door a young woman opened, did not react when I announced myself as Carlino but turned to pass the information to those inside. A voice told me to come in. In a grey-haired woman I did not recognize — although I knew it must be she — that Gina who had walked so bravely across the river and railway during the night when Ted and I were escorted to join the partisan group on Monte Morello. But the gaunt man who came in from the next room was undoubtedly Franco. We embraced. Slowly over the next days I learned how he had been denounced by someone in the village, arrested and sent to Verona for trial. Verona was the legal centre of Mussolini's Social Republic; its courts had condemned to death his son-in-law Ciano and those members of the Fascist Grand Council who had voted for his removal in July 1942 and were incautious enough to remain in his power. Here Franco was sentenced to twenty years imprisonment, to be served after the Axis victory. In the interim he would go to concentration camp in Mauthausen. He survived: one of a mere handful from the many Italians so condemned to return from deportation and imprisonment there. It was an experience that had left indelible marks on his body and mind. At last we could talk openly about the past and unravel mysteries; for in clandestinity

Pebbles from My Skull

neither of us had been open with the other. One mystery concerned precisely his placing of me with a family which, in social terms, had been dominant in village society and clearly not in any sense liberal. The answer was simple: he had gone to them in the knowledge of their past sympathy for the Fascist regime and had instructed them to accept me; which they had done because they could not, at that stage of the war, resist his political pressure and because I was a valuable pledge to be exchanged in the future. They were, however, not the only persons to be upset when I disappeared from the village: so too, it appears, were the Committee of National Liberation in Florence, who had given instructions that I was to be kept safely — no doubt for their own ends, perhaps to liaise with the Allies, perhaps to cross the lines with Franco, perhaps because they believed they might find my knowledge of Italian useful at some stage.

Together we walked through the village, meeting women who had mostly been girls when I was hidden there but talking also to the widow of a Fascist militiaman about the times when her husband, who had so startled Ted and me when we saw him in the street on our first morning, had guarded the railway tunnels in the valley. With Franco I climbed up to the farmhouse above the village where we had hidden in the barn and heard someone probe for us in the straw. Today it is a weekend and holiday home. We were photographed at the precise spot where he had confronted Ted and me and, with his hand in his pocket and his finger on the trigger of his revolver, had cross-questioned us in the dusk. From him I learned new things about the village. Walking from his fine new house to the old one in which I spent my first night in the village, we passed, in a re-entrant and somewhat detached from the rest of the houses, a tall building with closed green shutters. Did I know what it was? he asked. I had no idea. It was, he explained, the place where the rich men of the village — did that, I wondered, include the father of Diego and Ubaldo, who had been in the words of his widow so *signorile* as he

Afterword

drove along in his horse and trap — had kept their women, a sort of brothel set outside the limits of the community, hidden away in a fold of the hills. It cast a new light on village life, one that fitted well enough with the account of marriage customs in the village provided by Diego himself. Since last I was there his elderly wife — some sort of cousin — had died and he was married again, this time with children. He was himself unchanged with his ruddy face which, in profile, was that of Punchinello: a great nose and a strong curved chin. Marriage, he explained into a tape-recorder, had been arranged in this way: the family met and discussed the list of available women, what their property was, where it lay. It was advantageous, he explained, if the bride's property marched with one's own, or at least with the family's, and even more advantageous if she were herself a relative. In this way the chance of the property going out of the family was reduced. It was on these grounds that his first marriage had been arranged. All this he expounded with great clarity and naturalness. He did not explain the rationale of his second marriage. What became obvious was the edginess of his relationship to Franco Under the banter they exchanged I felt the cutting edge of old feuds. Sitting outside the cafe where the children ran in and out with ice creams or caramels, they argued, not so much about the events of the Second World War, as about things further back, under the Fascist regime — especially during the early days. Who, for instance, had fired the shot that killed some cousin of Diego's in the square by the church in 1923, or was it 1924? Who had beaten an anti-Fascist in the same square with the clubs that were the traditional weapon of the Blackshirt squads? It was a political bitterness that survived the social changes, the consumerism, the modern plumbing, the television sets, and the era of second homes for young married couples who drove up for a weekend in the cool of the hills away from the heat of Prato and the plain. It had roots clearly in Franco's own experience and, farther back yet, in that of his father. A man who had consistently refused to join the Fascist Party,

Pebbles from My Skull

he was set upon one night, beaten, dosed with castor oil and thrown naked into the kitchen in front of his wife and son. Perhaps it was this that led to a period in Franco's life, of which I had not heard before, when, as a boy, he and his father wandered south into Calabria, working as charcoal-burners, sleeping by their smoking conical pyramids, rising to tend the fire as the wolves howled beyond the flames in the darkness of the Sila plateau.

As we talked of the time we had been together, which was in fact remarkably short, Gina sat and listened, knitting on a canopied settee on the balcony above the road. She took little part in the recounting of incidents which she clearly knew by heart, only interrupting from time to time to correct a detail, to add a name, a date or a location. Where she had nothing to add was in his accounts of Mauthausen, of the quarries, of the guards who waited till a prisoner had toiled up to the top and then with a push sent him crashing down, along with his barrowload of stone, to death or mutilation on the boulders below. He had been fortunate enough to bluff his way into a work commando engaged on aeroplane maintenance; an Austrian woman had befriended him; he had survived and returned to confront the person who had betrayed him but whom he refused to identify, saying only that when they met in the village street (as was inevitable) he had said: 'I forbid you ever to speak to me again so long as you live.' Politically he had become withdrawn, perhaps disillusioned. On his return, which had clearly been a very difficult time both for him and Gina, he had been close to the Communist Party and had been invited to stand as a parliamentary deputy but he had confined himself to being active on the Prato town council, becoming progressively more independent and detached, a man haunted by the past.

One question he put to me. It was the same as readers and friends had posed. It concerned politics. There is in the original text, as they have rightly diagnosed, something in the nature of a political vacuum. It is true that they could deduce that I stood somewhere on the Left; but where

Afterword

precisely? and how deeply was I committed? Franco, too, had been puzzled in the course of our wartime contacts to know where to place me, partly because he found it difficult to conceive of a British officer as being of the Left. With him as with my readers I had been reticent: with him, because of the need to protect myself in a political situation in which I did not know his exact political position any more than he did mine; with my readers, because it would have been difficult for an executive of the BBC to admit that he had for some years been an active member of the Young Communist League and then of the Party, membership of which one was allowed to let lapse in wartime so that one could, with a clear conscience, declare to the military authorities that one was not a member of any political party. My reasons for joining the partisans were therefore quite specific and specifically political. Another void to which friends had pointed concerned the lack of sexual experience during my wanderings; which they found improbable. But during that period, although I found individual women attractive and although, given the absence of men, some of them might perhaps have been accessible, I remained always on the plane of friendship and that for two reasons: I did not wish to exploit a situation of trust and, more selfishly, I did not wish to add sexual complications to a situation already difficult enough. Besides, the experience of enforced chastity in a prisoner-of-war camp had made abstinence easier. It was, however, one of the disappointments of a previous visit to Italy, to the area of Chianti, that when I traced down that Maria for whom I had felt an almost brotherly affection she claimed not to remember me, an amnesia not shared by the rest of her family.

On this occasion I was visiting friends who had acquired a farmhouse in the heart of Chianti; it was, they wrote to me, almost certainly a house I would know. So it came that I sat drinking vermouth on the balcony of a house that looked across to the thickets of broom where, although I could no longer identify the exact spot, two German boys lie buried, one of them shot by myself. Here, as in the mountain

Pebbles from My Skull

village, things had changed greatly. The terraces in the vineyards had been blasted and bulldozed away so that instead of trellises running along the contours there were now concrete posts that marched up the slopes and over the tops of the hills. Agro-industry had arrived. It would exploit the hillsides for a few years, using mechanization to keep the ground clear of weeds, and bring fat profits to new proprietors who were German, Japanese, Swedish, British and who were content to see the topsoil wash away and fill the little river, which Dante described as red with blood, ankle-deep in red silt. The house at Le Granchiaie was derelict; the dam which once retained a stream in front of the house had been breached by the winter floods, which had undermined the banks, leaving a deep pit. The spring where the freshwater crabs that gave the place its name had bred was dry. Further up the valley the mill pond was empty and overgrown with grass and bushes. I prised the blue and white plate with the postal number of the house from the wall as a keepsake. The Tuscan peasants had gone; but in one farmhouse there was a Sardinian peasant and his family who made *pecorino* cheese. They were part of a wave of emigration from the poorer regions of Italy that was replacing some of the sharecroppers who had left the land to work in industry or to hire themselves out as labourers. The new land-owners were mostly foreigners. One — an English ex-officer married to an Italian *contessa* — came to invite my friends to a fiesta in a small town nearby. The Communist mayor was keen that foreigners should attend. 'Not a bad chap really, our little Communist,' he commented. So I saw them welcomed and toasted by the mayor. Outside posters urged solidarity with Chile. Such political cynicism cast a light for me on the desperation which had pushed some on the Left into terrorism with its tragic waste of life and its ironical result: the strengthening of the forces of repression within society. As I left I took with me, then, some understanding of why the partisan of today was likely to be the urban guerrilla, who had to be urban if only because, with the death of the peasant culture

Afterword

and the peasant networks on which I had depended for survival, the countryside would never again harbour a Maquis.

My family I located almost by chance. I had learned that they had moved some distance away from Le Granchiaie. One evening driving home with my friends I stopped on an impulse at a group of houses in the middle of the countryside in one of which there was a bar. Did anyone know the Mugelli family? I asked. Someone did. They lived about twenty minutes away. Quite close. Led by a guide we drove along a track that eventually, much later, led to a solitary and totally dark building. I was loath to disturb the inmates but the guide insisted. His beating on the door brought someone to open it — a man who, when the light fell on my face said: 'Carlino'. Inside we found his brother and his brother's wife. We exchanged greetings and then sat to talk, a conversation that developed into a cruel confrontation between two cultures, two ways of life, for the wife, turning to the doctor's wife and to my own inquired their ages. The question was put with great naturalness and interest. Before anyone could reply I knew what the outcome must be. For the age of the doctor's wife was that of the questioner; but whereas one was fresh of complexion and vigorous in her middle age the other bore in her whole being the marks of hardship and years of labour. The answer, which I had to translate, was like a blow. It was followed by a silence. Then the talk turned to other things and ended in an invitation to a peasant dinner a few days later at which once more I ate the traditional Tuscan fare of boiled and roast meat and drank the local Chianti. During the meal I sat next to the wife, who from time to time touched my arm and said to the company: '*E proprio lui*'. It's really him. Here it seems to me there was no sense in which I had been a possession but as the grandmother, now dead, had used to put it, another son.

It was during this stay in Chianti that a message came to me from the neighbouring village — from the local plumber — to the effect that he had known me during the

Pebbles from My Skull

war and would like my wife and me to come to supper. I did not recognize him— not unnaturally since in those days he had been a boy used as a messenger by the Resistance. We talked inevitably of the past. Then he revealed one of the reasons for his invitation. Did I remember, he asked, the young man I had had shot? He had thought that perhaps that death had remained with me and wished simply to tell me that they had discovered, after I had crossed the lines, that the boy had indeed been a spy. I was filled with wonder — and still am — at the sensibility, the understanding of human predicaments, that lay behind that announcement and his wish to lift from me a difficult memory. It leads me to reiterate what is I believe one of the most important discoveries I made during a time which was marked by many things that were difficult, frightening and painful: that in a world of cruelty and oppression there are still people who have generous impulses, courage and understanding. It is something that gives me, even in these dark and terrible times, when in so much of the world cruel and powerful forces have the ascendancy, a certain hope. It joins with the knowledge that in the most unexpected circumstances and at the most improbable conjunctures — for who would have thought that Mussolini's Italy, apparently so supine, would produce a resistance movement and a vast demonstration of political and human solidarity — the members of a society, of a class, undergo a transformation that endows them with courage and virtues beyond all possible expectation. Such moments, I think, happen relatively seldom in history — two or three times last century, four or five times in ours. They are part of that fight of which Benjamin said it is 'for the crude and material things without which no refined and spiritual things could exist . . . (but which) manifest themselves in this struggle as courage, humour, cunning and fortitude.' The Italians I knew, for the most part, displayed them to the full.